The Chartered Institute of Management Accountants

CIMA
PUBLISHING

Environmental Accounting for Sustainable Development

An Evaluation of Policy and Practice in the Forestry Sector in Cameroon

Charles Elad
University of Aberdeen

This publication arises from the research project 'Environmental Accounting for Sustainable Development: An Evaluation of Policy and Practice in the Forestry Sector in Cameroon' which was funded with a research grant from the CIMA Research Foundation. The award of a Research Foundation grant, and the publication of findings in this format, indicates that the recipient has successfully passed two separate peer review processes, which also involved practitioner assessors. The views expressed in this publication are the authors' own, and do not necessarily represent those of CIMA.

First published in 2000 by:
The Chartered Institute of Management Accountants
63 Portland Place
London
W1N 4AB

ISBN 1 85971 458 7

Contents

Abbreviations

AAC	African Accounting Council
ACCA	Association of Chartered Certified Accountants
ASB	Accounting Standards Board
ASC	Accounting Standards Committee
ASSC	Accounting Standards Steering Committee
BTN	Brussels Trade Nomenclature
CFA	Communauté Financière Africaine
CIMA	Chartered Institute of Management Accountants
CNAM	Conservatoire National des Arts et Métier, University of Paris
DSF	Déclaration Statistique et Fiscale
EU	European Union
FASB	Financial Accounting Standards Board
FOB	Free on board
FSC	Forest Stewardship Council
GATT	General Agreement on Tariffs and Trade
ha	Hectare
IASC	International Accounting Standards Committee
ISIC	International Standard Industrial Classification
NGO	Non Governmental Organisation
NPM	New Public Management
OCAM	Organisation Commune Africaine Malagache et Mauricienne
OHADA	Organisation pour l'Harmonisation en Afrique du Droit des Affaires
ONADEF	Office National de Développement des Forêts
ONECCA	Ordre National des Experts Comptables et des Comptables Agréés
PCG	Plan comptable général
SCAR-B	Système Comptable Africain de Référence de Base
SCS	Scientific Certification Systems Forest Conservation Programme
SEEC	Service d'Etudes Economiques du Cameroun
SGS	Société Générale de Surveillance
SIC	Standard Industrial Classification
SYSCOA	Système Comptable des pays de l'Afrique de l'Ouest
UDEAC	Union Douanière et Economique de l'Afrique Centrale
WTO	World Trade Organisation
WWF	World Wide Fund for Nature

Executive Summary

Introduction

The *Organisation Commune Africaine, Malagache et Mauricienne (OCAM) plan comptable général* (PCG) provides a robust accounting framework that seeks to integrate natural resource accounting (i.e. accounting for forestry and silvicultural products, wildlife, metals, chemicals, mineral resources etc.) within its cost accounting and financial reporting schemes.

The OCAM PCG has traditionally been used by the state as a tool to support environmental management, macroeconomic and fiscal policy decision making, performance evaluation and supervision of the activities of large transnational companies.

This study will address the following questions:

- To what extent has the government's strategy, whereby accounting is intertwined with economic development policy, stimulated sustainability in the forestry sector?
- How do management accountants in forestry companies restructure internal cost data to meet the environmental accounting and external reporting requirements of the OCAM PCG?
- To what extent have consumer-driven environmental audit and eco-labelling strategies enhanced sustainability in the forest industry?

Natural resource accounting and the conceptual framework of the OCAM plan

Although very little is known about it in the Anglo-Saxon world, the OCAM PCG was developed from a conceptual framework which was specifically structured to address the objectives of accounting and financial reporting in the developing countries concerned. Unlike the narrow 'decision usefulness' orientation of Anglo-Saxon conceptual frameworks – such as those developed by the ASB, IASC or FASB – the OCAM conceptual framework attempted to address the needs of a wide range of stakeholders.

Several variants of the OCAM PCG have evolved as a result of implementation bottlenecks in some countries.

The framework of the OCAM PCG compels companies to disclose information that is used to support environmental management. In particular, it incorporates extensive natural resource accounting information in volume/physical units and in monetary terms. This information can be used to monitor the rate of depletion of natural resources that can be attributed to the operations of large multinational companies.

Forestry policy and taxation

The framework of the OCAM PCG generates extensive segmental data, by geographical area and species of tree, which are used in forest tax calculations. The government also uses this information as a basis for granting tax concessions to companies in conformity with the Investment Code.

The forest tax statutes seek to alleviate some social justice problems by spelling out the modalities for allocating tax revenues to stakeholders such as village communities near logging sites, councils, central government, and a parastatal organisation that supposedly takes care of forest regeneration and management.

Forest tax rates over the period 1960-1994 were extremely low and resulted in the expropriation of natural resources by foreign multinational companies. This problem was, to a large extent, reversed by recent reforms in the 1995 Finance Law.

Auditing in the forest industry

In recent years, a number of forest management audit schemes have evolved as a means of striking the right balance between the development requirements of rural people whose livelihood is inextricably linked to the forests; the macroeconomic objectives of the government who need to procure income from timber; and, not least, environmental campaigners, activist groups, and non-governmental organisations who want to protect the forests.

The Forest Stewardship Council (FSC) was established in 1993 as an independent private sector organisation charged with the development of forest auditing standards and the accreditation of auditors who certify the quality of forest management.

The impact of FSC auditing standards on governance arrangements in the forestry sector was analysed using a case study of Leroy Gabon, a large Franco-German logging concession in the Congo Basin rainforest. Some of the key findings can be summarised as follows:

- Consumer-driven forest management audits sanctioned by the FSC could shift much of the responsibility for sustainable forest management from state bureaucracy to management control mechanisms within forest exploitation companies, in line with the New Public Management agenda.
- Many of the problems associated with financial audit procedures also arise in FSC-based audits.
- In some respects, the FSC eco-labelling scheme could be seen as part of a strategic posture adopted by a company to defend its enlightened self interests.

Evaluation of policy and practice

The OCAM model, coupled with the FSC auditing scheme, offers an approach to the problem of costing environmental sustainability that complements the theoretical framework adopted in the Landcare experimental project in New Zealand.

The conceptual framework of the OCAM PCG takes care of the following key questions that are also considered in ongoing ACCA and IASC projects on accounting in developing countries:

- Should there be a close link between accounting and tax reporting?
- To what extent is the accounting model appropriate to users other than investors in private companies?
- Are the economies in developing countries biased toward certain industries which are less important in developed countries (e.g. agriculture, forestry, extractive industries, etc)?
- Should there be industry-specific standards?
- Should the accounting system be based on procedural standards and guidelines similar to the French *plan comptable?*

1

Introduction

1.1 Background to the study

In 1991, the Law and Parliamentary Committee of the Chartered Institute of Management Accountants (CIMA) commissioned a study on the wider social and economic benefits of uniform accounting systems. The main outcome of this project was a research report entitled *Financial Reporting in Europe: The Management Interface,* which arrived at the conclusion that UK companies could benefit from adoption of a uniform chart of accounts based on the French *plan comptable général* model for internal data codification and classification purposes (CIMA, 1991; Likierman, 1992a, 1992b). Although a number of studies have documented these desirable features of French accounting, it is not widely recognised in the English-speaking world that the Organisation Commune Africaine Malagache et Mauricienne (OCAM) *plan comptable général* (hereafter PCG), a forerunner of the 1982 French PCG, provides an even more robust accounting framework that seeks to integrate topical issues such as natural resource accounting (i.e. accounting for forestry and silvicultural products, wildlife, metals, chemicals, mineral resources etc.) within its cost accounting and financial reporting system.

It will be demonstrated in this research report that, in Cameroon, this accounting model has traditionally been used by the government as a tool to support environmental management, macroeconomic planning, fiscal policy decision-making, performance evaluation and supervision of the activities of large transnational companies. In particular, there is a unique linkage between the wide range of environmental and social accounting disclosures generated by the OCAM PCG and a package of tax incentives which are granted in conformity with the Investment Code. However, to date, no study has been carried out to assess the extent to which this arrangement has stimulated sustainable economic development.

Accordingly, the main objective of this study is to evaluate the extent to which the government's strategy whereby accounting is intertwined with economic development policy has stimulated sustainability in the forestry sector.

1.2 Importance to CIMA

The importance of this study to CIMA as an international accountancy body is mainly in terms of:

- The need to develop the issues raised in the CIMA report entitled *Financial Reporting in Europe: The Management Interface,* and in particular, the way in which management accountants in OCAM countries restructure internal cost data to meet the environmental accounting and external reporting requirements of the uniform OCAM Accounting Plan.

- The need to evaluate ongoing projects on accounting in developing countries that are carried out under the auspices of the International Accounting Standards Committee, the ACCA, and the United Nations group of experts on accounting (see Nobes, 1998, for details).

- The need to protect the Cameroon rainforest which comprises millions of acres of high-quality wood such as mahogany, ebony, and teak among a wide range of other rare trees which portray a pattern based on natural selection. This forest is also home to abundant fauna which include gorillas, lions, chimpanzees and elephants. The importance of this forest to other countries can be seen in terms of its symbiotic relationship with the global environment and also in terms of scientific interests. For example, almost every paper that appeared in the 1996 proceedings of the Royal Society of Edinburgh (Section B, Biological Sciences) made reference to aspects of the Cameroon rainforest (Alexander et al., 1996).

1.3 Context of the study

As Gray (1995) observed, the notion of sustainability has opened up new debates across the social sciences. The bulk of prior accounting research in this area was carried out in the context of the industrialised countries where the head offices of most transnational corporations are located. This point was noted by Gray and Kouhy (1993, p.388):

> At first sight, the whole consideration of environmental accounting for LDCs [less developed countries] seems quite bizarre. In the first place, from a global environmental perspective, the relative global environmental degradation created by LDCs, as opposed to that created by developed, or perhaps 'over-developed' countries [ODCs hereafter] is relatively trivial in all but one or two areas – notably rainforests and deserts.

The above citation provides a strong case for confining the scope of the current study to the forestry sector in Cameroon, which is dominated by over 150 European logging companies (Vidal, 1990; Elad and Gray, 1991). This point also highlights the importance of the symbiotic relationship between the tropical forest in LDCs and the global environment which includes that of the ODCs.

Prior research on accounting for sustainability can be classified broadly into four main categories, namely: (i) theoretical papers that draw on the social accounting and/or radical accounting literature (e.g. Ullmann, 1976; Maunders and Burritt, 1991; Gray, 1992); (ii) analysis of environmental disclosures in corporate reports (e.g. Roberts, 1991); (iii) surveys of accountants' attitudes (e.g. Bebbington, Gray,

Thomson and Walters, 1994), and (iv) papers that deal with measurement issues (e.g. Dey et al., 1995; Bebbington and Tan, 1996). Although it is obviously difficult to pigeon-hole papers neatly into these categories, the present study falls substantially within the fourth category since it seeks to assess the way in which the OCAM PCG has tackled some of the measurement issues raised in the theoretical model for costing sustainability proposed by Bebbington and Tan (1996).

1.4 Content of the report

Chapter 2 of this report presents a critical analysis and appraisal of the evolutionary history and conceptual framework of the OCAM Plan, particularly in the context of the member states of the *Union Douanière et Economique de L'Afrique Centrale* (UDEAC, i.e. Customs and Economic Union of Central Africa).

Chapter 3 analyses the way in which the framework of the OCAM PCG dovetails into a standard industrial classification which incorporates a taxonomy of forest resources, chemicals, metals, minerals, and other natural resources. In particular, the use of the OCAM Plan as a tool to support fiscal policy, macroeconomic planning and sustainable forest management is explained.

Chapter 4 looks at forestry taxation, while Chapter 5 focuses exclusively on forest stewardship audit and corporate governance. Finally, in Chapter 6, the key issues in earlier chapters are drawn together in order to: (i) show how the OCAM approach complements the theoretical model for costing environmental sustainability proposed by Bebbington and Tan (1996), and (ii) evaluate the OCAM Plan's conceptual framework against the backdrop of an ongoing IASC project on accounting in developing countries.

References

Alexander, I, Swaine, M and Walting, R (eds) (1996), *Proceedings of the Royal Society of Edinburgh,* Section B, Biological Sciences, Vol. 104.

Bebbington, J, Gray, R, Thomson, I and Walters, D (1994) 'Accountants' Attitudes and Environmentally-sensitive Accounting', *Accounting and Business Research,* Vol. 24, No. 94, pp. 109–20.

Bebbington, J and Tan, J (1996), 'Accounting for Sustainability', *Chartered Accountants Journal,* July, pp. 75–6.

Chartered Institute of Management Accountants (1991), *Financial Reporting in Europe: The Management Interface,* London, CIMA.

Dey, C, Evans, R and Gray, R H (1995), 'Towards Social Information Systems and Bookkeeping: A Note on Developing the Mechanisms for Social Accounting and Audit', *Journal of Applied Accounting Research,* Vol. 2, No. 3, pp. 36–69.

Elad, C M and Gray, S J (1991), 'Value Added Accounting in Equatorial Africa', Paper presented at the 1991 Congress of the European Accounting Association, University of Limburg, Maastricht, The Netherlands.

Gray, R H (1992), 'Accounting and Environmentalism: An Exploration of the Challenge of Gently Accounting for Accountability, Transparency and Sustainability', *Accounting, Organisations and Society,* 17:5, pp. 399–425.

Gray, R H (1995), 'Social and Environmental Accounting Research', Briefings from the GEC Programme, *Global Environmental Change Programme Briefings,* No. 5, September.

Gray, R H and Kouhy, R (1993), 'Accounting for the Environment and Sustainability in Lesser Developed Countries: An Exploratory Note', *Research in Third World Accounting,* Vol. 2, pp. 387–99.

Likierman, A (1992a), 'Plaidoyer anglais pour un système à la française', *Revue Française de Comptabilité,* May.

Likierman, A (1992b), 'A Case for the French Connection', *The Times,* 30 January, p. 27.

Maunders, K and Burritt R (1991), 'Accounting and Ecological Crisis', *Accounting, Auditing and Accountability Journal,* 4:3, pp. 9–26.

Nobes, C (1998), *Accounting in Developing Economies: Questions about Users, Uses and Appropriate Reporting Practices,* London, ACCA.

Roberts, C B (1991), 'Environmental Disclosures: A Note on Reporting Practices in Europe, Accounting and Ecological Crisis', *Accounting, Auditing and Accountability Journal,* 4:3, pp. 62–71.

Ullmann, A (1976), 'The Corporate Environmental Accounting System: A Management Tool for Fighting Environmental Degradation', *Accounting, Organisations and Society,* 1:1, pp.71–9.

Vidal, J (1990), 'New Gods in the Jungle – Cameroon Rainforests', *Guardian,* 2 March, p. 21.

2

Conceptual Framework of the OCAM Plan

2.1 Introduction

Comparative international accounting research has shown that different accounting patterns have evolved in different parts of the world in response to a variety of economic, social, institutional and cultural factors. However, most developing countries do not have indigenous accounting systems. Furthermore, it may not be appropriate for these countries to emulate the Anglo-Saxon accounting models which are biased toward external financial reporting and which largely de-emphasise the managerial and socio-economic dimensions of accounting.

The International Accounting Standards Committee (IASC) was mindful of this criticism when it commissioned a project on accounting issues that are relevant to the environmental settings of developing countries. The terms of reference for this project include the following tentative list of key questions that need to be addressed (Nobes, 1988, p.10):

(a) Should IASC develop a basic system of accounting – procedural standards and guidelines similar to the French *plan comptable* – for developing countries?
(b) Should there be different accounting standards or different disclosure standards for enterprises in developing countries and countries in transition?
(c) Should IASC develop industry-specific standards that will be particularly relevant for these countries, in addition to the current projects on agriculture, extractive industries and insurance?
(d) Should IASC develop a standard on accounting for joint ventures (which is now dealt with in IAS 31)?
(e) Should IASC develop guidelines on accounting for privatisation, including changes in accounting entities, changes in accounting systems, and valuation in cases where no evidence of comparable transactions exists?
(f) Should IASC adopt standards or guidelines on bartering?
(g) Are there any special problems with applying existing IAS in developing countries or countries in transition? Examples cited include segment disclosures, related-party disclosures, foreign exchange rate controls, and hyperinflationary economies.

In this chapter, it will be made evident that, although very little is known about it in the Anglo-Saxon world, the OCAM Accounting Plan was developed from a conceptual framework for accounting in developing countries which also tackled questions (a), (b), and (c) above. Interestingly, the emphasis on these three questions ties in well with the views of Nobes (1998, p. 40) when he argues that the IASC does not need to pay much attention to issues (d) to (g). The need to address these questions was well articulated in the foreword to the Plan by the OCAM Secretary-General (OCAM, 1973, p.VII) as the key motivation behind the accounting plan project:

> 'The need for information in economic planning has led the OCAM Heads of State and Government to decide that a study should be made on the standardisation of accounting methods applicable to agricultural, industrial and commercial businesses.'

A review of the evolutionary history of the OCAM Plan is provided in the next section. Subsequent sections present a critical analysis and appraisal of the Plan's conceptual framework.

2.2 OCAM, UDEAC and accounting harmonisation in Central Africa

OCAM was formed in 1965 as a regional organisation representing the following Francophone African states: Cameroon, Gabon, Central African Republic, Chad, Congo, Ivory Coast, Senegal, Benin, Togo, Upper Volta (Burkina Faso), Mauritania, Niger, Burundi, French Somalia (Djibouti), Zaïre, Dahomey, Mali, Madagascar and Mauritius. Its objective was to promote economic, social and technical co-operation and its formation was strongly supported by France. Although many member states withdrew from the organisation during the 1970s, the greatest legacy of OCAM is the common Accounting Plan.

The OCAM Accounting Plan still has a tremendous impact on accounting throughout Francophone Africa. The Plan was developed from a well-structured and systematic planning programme over a four-year period. The idea of developing a common accounting system commensurate with local environmental needs was spearheaded by the UDEAC member states, which felt acutely that the accounting systems which had been imposed on them by colonial powers were inappropriate. In response to this initiative, a conference of OCAM Heads of State was convened in Niamey (Niger) in 1968 where the matter was discussed and approved. The Secretary-General of OCAM was immediately entrusted with the task of formulating a strategy and schedule for the development of a new accounting system that would befit the needs of member states. The main stages in the historical development of the OCAM Plan outlined in OCAM (1973) are summarised in Table 2.1.

Table 2.1 Schedule for the OCAM Accounting Plan Project

December 1967	UDEAC member states asked that a General Accounting Plan adapted to their environmental needs for business management and national economic planning be drawn up.
January 1968	Heads of OCAM states met in Niamey and approved the idea of an accounting plan which would be common to all member states. The OCAM Secretary-General was entrusted with the task of preparing a timetable and co-ordinating the preliminary studies necessary for the formulation and adoption of the General Accounting Plan.
January 1969	Resolution passed at a planning meeting in Kinshasa stressing the need to execute the project without delay.
October 1969	Workshop for OCAM statisticians and economic planners held in Yaoundé to analyse the objectives and design of the Plan.
1969 to 1970	Fiscal and statistical experts drawn from the OCAM countries meet at Lomé to discuss and appraise the blueprint of the OCAM Accounting Plan. A blueprint of the OCAM Accounting Plan was circulated among government officials and private-sector representatives of member states for discussion and comment.
January 1970	The OCAM Accounting Plan was officially adopted by Heads of State at a summit meeting in Yaoundé, where a resolution was passed for immediate implementation of the provisions of the Plan.

2.3 Conceptual framework of the OCAM Plan

There is a general tendency to visualise the idea of a conceptual framework for accounting only in terms of documents originating from the Anglo-Saxon world which were formally constituted as such. It can be argued, however, that the OCAM project[1] was an attempt to develop a conceptual framework for accounting in developing nations. An outline of the conceptual framework which constituted the terms of reference guiding those responsible for the formulation and implementation of the OCAM Plan is set out in Figure 2.1. It indicates that, in several respects, the OCAM project was very much in tune with the spirit of the British *Corporate Report* (ASSC, 1975), the Canadian *Stamp Report* (CICA, 1980) and the *Trueblood Report* (AICPA, 1973). One important feature which these documents have in common is that, by and large, they all address the objectives of accounting and financial reporting in their respective countries. For example, the aims of the *Trueblood Report* were to determine:

1 Although very little is known about it in the Anglo-Saxon world, the OCAM Plan is generally recognised as one of the most important achievements of French/Francophone accounting. Giscard d'Estaing, a former French president who, at the time, was minister of finance, has been quoted as saying that the OCAM Plan is one of the most successful documents of its kind and that it has influenced accounting practice in several countries around the world (Kinzonzi, 1984, p. 271). Versions of the Plan now exist in several languages, including English, Spanish and Japanese. Courses on the OCAM Plan are taught at the Conservatoire National des Arts et Métier, University of Paris (CNAM, 1994).

(i) who needs financial statements?
(ii) what information do they need?
(iii) how much of the needed information can be provided through accounting?
(iv) what framework is required to provide the needed information?

Figure 2.1 Conceptual framework of the OCAM Plan

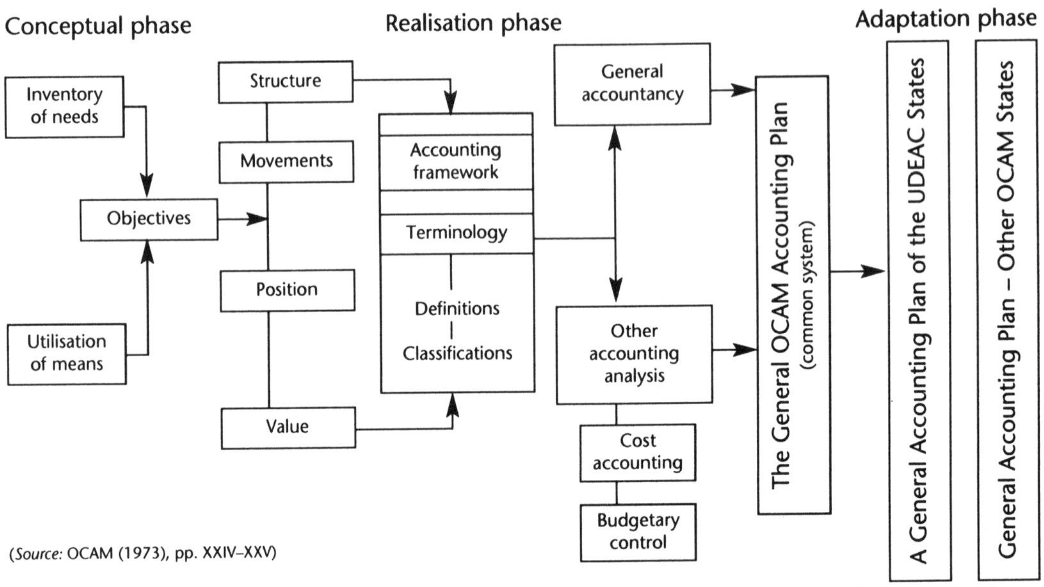

(*Source:* OCAM (1973), pp. XXIV–XXV)

The three phases in the OCAM project shown in Figure 2.1 (conceptual phase, realisation phase and adaptation phase) are clearly in line with the Trueblood aims listed above. For instance, objectives (i) and (ii) in the Trueblood list correspond to the OCAM 'inventory of needs'. Similarly, 'utilisation of means' in OCAM corresponds to objective (iii) in Trueblood. Finally, objective (iv) in Trueblood may correspond to the entire OCAM 'realisation phase'.

As such, there are reasonable grounds for the argument that the OCAM project was the first ever attempt to develop a conceptual framework for accounting in developing countries. The search for a conceptual framework for accounting normally involves a sequential process. It begins with the definition of the objectives of accounting and ends with the derivation of a 'constitution' or the conceptual framework proper which could be used to develop accounting standards and guide practice (FASB, 1976; Macve, 1981; Belkaoui, 1986). To date, no generally accepted conceptual framework has been produced. Documents such as the *Trueblood Report,* the *Corporate Report* and the *Stamp Report* only constitute a first step towards the attainment of this goal since they are largely concerned with the objectives of accounting. Although the FASB's project is by far the most advanced conceptual framework, it has not succeeded in protecting the public interest or in resolving all standard-setting problems. Like most other conceptual framework documents (e.g. the ASB *Statement of Principles*), the FASB conceptual framework's narrow emphasis on 'decision usefulness' makes it deficient in that it focuses largely on the requirements of investors and creditors as opposed to those of other stakeholders.

The introductory pages of the OCAM Plan provide a description of the three major phases in Figure 2.1. As is the case with the *Corporate Report,* a wide range of users and their information needs are identified here. These include businessmen, investors, economic planners, Inland Revenue authorities, management, ministries of education (for teaching and professional training) and other third parties, including stock exchanges, bankers, creditors, financial analysts and so on.

The Plan acknowledges that user needs may not be homogeneous across user groups. It also acknowledges that it would be difficult to satisfy adequately the information needs of all the groups alike. In view of this problem, the approach taken by the Plan was to prescribe very detailed disclosures for general-purpose corporate reports. The aim was to meet the conceivable needs of all the major user groups. This was specifically expressed in OCAM (1973, p. XV):

> If a list of all the needs of these different users were compiled, it will have to be admitted that each party has a scale of preference for the economic information desired, but nonetheless, all information of this kind comes from a common stock ... a collection of elementary facts which, if extracted with accuracy, precision and consistency will with appropriate treatment give satisfaction to all users.

Several empirical studies on user needs or the importance of disclosures which were conducted long after the OCAM Plan was designed have also reached the conclusion that various user groups have different scales of preferences for accounting information (Baker and Haslem, 1973; Buzby, 1974; Firth, 1978; Belkaoui and Kahl, 1978; Wallace, 1988).

The conceptual phase outlined in Figure 2.1 ends with a formal statement of the objectives to be pursued by the OCAM Plan. These were stated as follows in OCAM (1973, p. XVI):

(1) The quest for an accounting system that will find acceptance by and be suitable for all users.
(2) The standardisation of accounting systems at the level of the most general analysis.
(3) The adaptation of accounting methods to modern means of data processing.
(4) Proper teaching and training of accountants.

Objective (1) of the OCAM conceptual framework stated above has not been achieved in practice. The experiences of the industrialised Western countries have shown that it is virtually impossible to develop an accounting system that would be acceptable to all user/non-user groups (or stakeholders), for several reasons. For example, the economic consequences of accounting standardisation may cause user groups or stakeholders to perceive the usefulness of accounting principles from different perspectives. This may hinder the prospects for unanimous acceptance (Zeff and Keller, 1985; Rappaport, 1985). Hence, accounting policy-making is essentially a political and social process with some bargaining among competing interest groups. This clearly constitutes an impediment to the achievement of 'neutrality', an essential qualitative characteristic enunciated in most conceptual framework documents (Solomons, 1978; Horngren, 1985; Peasnell, 1982; Elad, 1998). Objective (4) is vital for successful accounting harmonisation since it will facilitate the adoption and implementation of the Plan. The introduction of courses on the OCAM Plan at secondary school and university level as well as vocational and other professional programmes will produce the necessary personnel who would foster its adoption and implementation. In Cameroon, this has prompted the authorities to undertake radical educational reforms by introducing OCAM-based courses at all levels (secondary/vocational and tertiary).

In the realisation phase, the basic accounting concepts and conventions to be adopted for the attainment of the Plan's objectives are identified. It is pointed out in this part of the document that these conventions include well-established and generally accepted fundamental accounting concepts such as prudence, consistency, accruals and so on. It is also stated that some features of the French *plans comptables* of 1947 and 1957 were used in the establishment of a uniform terminology and precise definition/classification of account codes. The authors of the Plan stated that these features were incorporated into its design to the extent that they combine simplicity and logic with flexibility and also leave room for further development. For instance, it was indicated that cost accounting and budgetary control which have not yet been dealt with comprehensively, are potential areas for further development.

Finally, the adaptation phase allows minor amendments to the main provisions of the Plan. These may relate to unavoidable variations in regional or national laws, taxation or accounting policy matters such as the requirement for compulsory revaluation of fixed assets over a specified period. Recommended practices in respect of such matters might vary among the OCAM and UDEAC countries.

2.4 The OCAM Plan and the evolution of accounting systems in Africa

Several impediments to the implementation of the OCAM Plan have been encountered in practice. These include variations in the resources and institutional settings of the countries concerned, such as the availability of qualified accountants, number and size distribution of companies, shareholders, educational resources and effective regulatory mechanisms. These impediments appear to have triggered the evolution of several variants of the OCAM Plan across the continent. For instance, in the Ivory Coast (an OCAM country with a stock exchange) a much simpler version of the Plan with fewer disclosures which de-emphasises its macroeconomic bias has evolved.

Figure 2.2 A judgemental classification of accounting systems in Africa

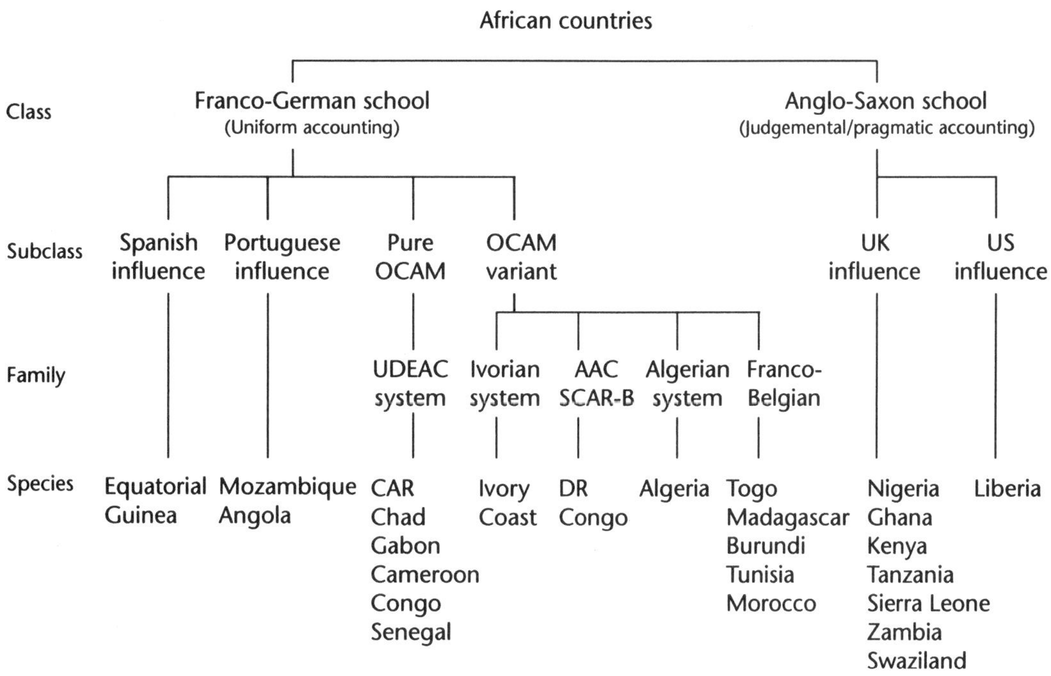

Enthoven (1977, p. 209) and Kinzonzi (1984) report that the Ivorian variant is less statistical and more financially oriented than the original version. The latest variants include the 'Système Comptable Africain de Référence de Base' (SCAR-B) which was developed by the African Accounting Council; the Système Comptable des pays de l'Afrique de l'Ouest (SYSCOA) which was designed for implementation in French-speaking West Africa in 1998; and the Organisation pour l'Harmonisation en Afrique du Droit des Affaires (OHADA) model which has not yet been implemented (see, for example, Causse, 1999, pp.218-219; Corinne, 1999). Others are indicated in the judgemental classification of accounting patterns in Africa given in Figure 2.2, which was developed by Elad (1998) based upon the analyses of Nobes (1983) and Kinzonzi (1984).

This study is mainly concerned with the pure version of the OCAM Plan as adopted by the member states of UDEAC, namely Cameroon, Gabon, Congo, Chad, Central African Republic and Equatorial Guinea. These countries belong to the Franc Zone and have a common central bank and currency (the CFA franc) which is pegged to the French franc. Accounting harmonisation and regulation are important by-products of economic integration in the UDEAC subregion. Public accountants and accounting firms can only obtain their authorisation and licences to practise as statutory auditors or *commissaires aux comptes* from the Union's management committee (UDEAC, 1970). Registered practitioners use the designation *Expert Comptable Agréé par l'UDEAC.*

There is also a regional code for foreign direct investment by multinational companies (UNCTC, 1988, p. 343; Letenou, 1988, pp. 28–9) and all member states are subject to the same supranational accounting regulatory framework. The management committee of UDEAC is responsible for accounting regulation in the entire sub-region. For example, Act No. 4-70-UDEAC-133 of 1970 states that no person shall bear the title of licensed accountant or exercise such profession unless he/she has been authorised by an Act of the management committee of UDEAC. Further, Act No. 5-82-UDEAC-324 of 1982 defines the rights and duties of auditors. All company audit reports make reference to these Acts in addition to the French commercial law of 1806 which is still enforced. Another example of regional regulation is Act No.7-82-UDEAC-362 of 1982 which harmonises financial reporting by banks and financial institutions in member states.

Each member state has its own domestic mechanism for enforcement of UDEAC pronouncements. In Cameroon, the Permanent Secretariat for the OCAM/UDEAC Accounting Plan in the Ministry of Economy and Planning and the Department of Taxation (Ministry of Finance) are responsible for the implementation of UDEAC accounting regulations. They effectively act as a liaison between the national environment and the UDEAC management committee.

A private-sector professional body, the *Ordre National des Experts Comptables et des Comptables Agréés du Cameroun* (ONECCA), was formed in 1985. However, the preamble to its constitution clearly states that it shall be governed by all previous and subsequent UDEAC Acts. This means that it has no authority to license potential entrants to the profession or influence accounting practice except in liaison with the UDEAC management committee.

The Department of Statistics (Ministry of Economy and Planning) has groups of statistical engineers and technicians at each provincial capital who meticulously check all annual reports submitted for onward transmission to its head office in Yaoundé. This means that reports which do not comply with UDEAC pronouncements will be rejected automatically at the provincial level. The Department of Statistics also plays an advisory role on accounting matters by organising training courses for practitioners or else dispatching staff to companies (in cases of non-compliance) to explain appropriate OCAM accounting principles. Delesalle (1987), a French professor who spent several years working in Cameroon as an adviser on the accounting plan *(Animateur Plan Comptable)* at the Department of Statistics in Douala, makes the following observation in a French accounting journal (p. 11): 'In Cameroon, after thirteen years of implementation, one might note that this reform has been well received and that the adoption of the OCAM plan is widespread' [author's translation].

2.5 Summary of key points

- The OCAM Plan was the first ever attempt by a group of developing countries to construct (albeit with French technical assistance) an accounting system primarily designed to meet their own information needs.
- Although some commentators (e.g. Wallace, 1990, p. 44) claim that no study has addressed issues such as a conceptual framework within the context of developing countries, this chapter has shown that the OCAM project was a conceptual framework project for accounting in the developing countries concerned.

- Several variants of the OCAM PCG have emerged in many Francophone and Lusophone countries.
- Many of the key questions that are currently being considered by the IASC's project on relevant accounting issues for developing countries and countries in transition were taken into account in the design of the OCAM PCG.

References

Accounting Standards Steering Committee (1975), *The Corporate Report,* London, ASSC.

American Institute of Certified Public Accountants (1973), *Report of the Study Group on the Objectives of Financial Statements – The Trueblood Report,* New York, AICPA.

Baker, H K and Haslem, J (1973), 'Information Needs of Individual Investors', *Journal of Accountancy,* 136, November, pp. 64–9.

Belkaoui, A (1986), *Accounting Theory,* New York, Harcourt Brace Jovanovich.

Belkaoui, A and Kahl, A (1978), *Corporate Financial Disclosure in Canada,* Vancouver, Canadian Certified General Accountants Association.

Buzby, S (1974), 'Selected Items of Information and their Disclosure in Annual Reports', *Accounting Review,* XLIX, pp. 423–35.

Causse, G (1999), 'Vingt Ans de Normalisation Comptable et de PCG. Son Influence dans les Pays de l'Afrique Francophone', *Comptabilité-Contrôle-Audit,* May, pp. 211–22.

Canadian Institute of Chartered Accountants (1980), *Corporate Reporting: Its Future Evolution,* Toronto, CICA.

CNAM (1994), *Institut National des Techniques Economiques et Comptables, Edition 1994–1995 avec Dossier d'Inscription,* INTEC, Ministère de l'Enseignement Supérieure et de la Recherche, Paris, Conservatoire National des Arts et Métiers.

Corinne, O (1999), 'Les normes comptables dans les pays d'Afrique', *Révue Française de Comptabilité,* 313, July-August, pp. 60–71.

Delesalle, E (1987), 'Le fait comptable au Cameroun', *L'Expert Comptable de Demain, France,* June, pp. 7–13.

Elad, C M 1998), 'Corporate Disclosure Regulation and Practice in the Developing Countries of Central Africa', *Advances in Public Interest Accounting,* Vol. 7, pp. 51–106.

Enthoven, A J H (1977), *Accountancy Systems in Third World Economies,* Amsterdam, North-Holland Publishing.

Financial Accounting Standards Board (1976), *Conceptual Framework for Financial Accounting and Reporting: Elements of Financial Statements and their Measurement,* New York, FASB.

Firth, M (1978), 'A Study on the Consensus of the Perceived Importance of Disclosure of Individual Items in Company Annual Reports', *International Journal of Accounting Education and Research,* 14, No. 1, pp. 57–70.

Horngren, C (1985), 'Uses and Limitations of a Conceptual Framework', in S A Zeff and T F Keller (eds), *Financial Accounting Theory: Issues and Controversies,* New York, McGraw-Hill, pp. 120–6.

Kinzonzi, M N K (1984), *Normalisation Comptable: Facteur d'Accélération du Développement Economique,* Paris, Foucher.

Kinzonzi, M N K (1986), 'The role of the African Accounting Council', in *Harmonisation of Accounting Standards* – Achievements and Prospects, Paris, OECD, pp. 109–13.

Letenou, E (1988), 'Comment solliciter un agrément au code des investissements', *Le Reflet,* Douala, Cameroon Chamber of Commerce, April/May, pp. 26–9.

Macve, R (1981), *A Conceptual Framework for Financial Accounting and Reporting,* London, ICAEW.

Nobes, C W (1983), 'A Judgemental International Classification of Financial Reporting Practice', *Journal of Business Finance and Accounting,* 10, pp. 1–19.

Nobes, C W (1988), 'Major International Differences in Financial Reporting', in C W Nobes and R H Parker (eds), *Issues in Multinational Accounting,* Oxford, Philip Allan, pp. 43–61.

Nobes, C W (1998), *Accounting in Developing Economies: Qestions about Users, Uses and Appropriate Reporting Practices,* London, ACCA.

OCAM (1973), *OCAM General Accounting Plan – Joint Organisation of African, Malagasy and Mauritian States,* Paris, OCAM.

Peasnell, K V (1982), 'The Functions of a Conceptual Framework for Corporate Financial Reporting', *Accounting and Business Research,* 12, pp. 243–56.

Rappaport, A (1985), 'Economic Impact of Accounting Standards – Implications for the FASB', in S A Zeff and T F Keller (eds), *Financial Accounting Theory: Issues and Controversies,* New York, McGraw-Hill, pp. 127–39.

Solomons, D (1978), 'The Politicization of Accountancy', *Journal of Accountancy,* 146, November, pp. 65–72.

UDEAC (1970), 'Act No. 4-70-UDEAC-133', *Internal Regulations of the Ordre Nationale des Experts Comptables et des Comptables Agréés du Cameroun,* Douala, ONECCA.

UDEAC (1982), 'Act No. 7-82-UDEAC-362', *Internal Regulations of the Ordre Nationale des Experts Comptables et des Comptables Agréés du Cameroun,* Douala, ONECCA.

UDEAC (1982), 'Act No. 5-82-324 of 18 December', *Journal Officiel de la République Unie du Cameroun.*

United Nations Centre on Transnational Companies (1988), *Transnational Corporations in World Development: Trends and Prospects,* New York, UNCTC.

Wallace, R S O (1988), 'Intranational and International Consensus on the Importance of Disclosure Items in Financial Reports: a Nigerian Case Study', *British Accounting Review,* 20, pp. 223–65.

Wallace, R S O (1990), 'Accounting in Developing Countries: A Review of the Literature', *Research in Third World Accounting,* 1, pp. 3–54.

Zeff, S A and Keller, T F (eds) (1985), *Financial Accounting Theory: Issues and Controversies,* New York, McGraw-Hill.

3

Natural Resource Accounting and the OCAM Plan

This chapter analyses the way in which the framework of the OCAM Plan dovetails into a taxonomy of local trees and a standard industrial classification that covers wildlife, chemicals, metals, minerals and other natural resources. In particular, the way in which the OCAM Plan has been used as a tool to support sustainable forest management, fiscal policy decision-making, and macroeconomic planning by the state is brought to bear.

3.1 The framework of the OCAM Accounting Plan

The OCAM Accounting Plan was formulated in the late 1960s and developed from the French *plans comptables* of 1947 and 1957 which most OCAM member states inherited from colonial rule. The Plan was first published by the French Ministry of Co-operation in January 1970, and was subsequently revised in 1980 and in 1988 (*Revue Française de Comptabilité*, 1988). The system of comprehensive decimal coding for principal accounts was retained. However, there were major innovations in the OCAM Plan – namely, the introduction of new financial statements such as the funds statement, a modular income statement incorporating separate sections for gross profit and value added, requirements for consolidation, the compulsory inclusion of notes to the accounts, and the disclosure of accounting policies. None of the aforementioned items had ever been featured in any of the French *plans comptables* up to the time the OCAM Plan was formulated. Presumably, the French technocrats who provided technical advice on the design of the OCAM Plan were less constrained in Francophone Africa than in France. Some authors (e.g. Beeny, 1976, p. 45; Forrester, 1983; Capelle, 1986; Kinzonzi, 1984) have suggested that the French have had to catch up with some of the innovations in the OCAM Plan when they adopted the European Union Fourth Directive in their revised 1982 *plan comptable*. The framework of the OCAM Plan comprises ten principal account codes as follows:

Balance sheet accounts (five classes)

Class one	Capital and long-term liabilities
Class two	Fixed and long-term assets
Class three	Stock
Class four	Third-party and adjustment accounts
Class five	Financial accounts

Income statement (three classes)

Class six	Expenses
Class seven	Revenue
Class eight	Results of main operations

Cost accounts (one class)

Class nine

Static accounts (one class)

Class zero	Extraordinary items
	Non-operating items
	All balance sheet account items

As in most *plans comptables,* each of the principal codes listed above is broken down into further sub-codes within each class, sometimes running up to ten digits. A preceding zero in any code means that the account in question has class zero properties in addition to those attributed to its other digits. The plan defines the criteria for assigning further digits, say, to differentiate between domestic and foreign sales or a wide range of other segmental data by line of business and geographical area. Issues relating to segmental reporting are now considered in greater depth.

3.2 Segmental reporting

One of the major problems encountered by legislators and accounting standard setting bodies dealing with segmental disclosures relates to the definition of what constitutes a reportable segment. This matter was raised by Emmanuel and Gray (1978) who pointed out that neither the British Companies Acts, the EC nor OECD segmental reporting pronouncements actually define a segment. They proposed that the Standard Industrial Classification (SIC) be considered as an important basis for segment identification. It is interesting to note that this approach had already been prescribed by the OCAM Accounting Plan.

In Cameroon, the authorities have operationalised the segmental reporting provisions of the OCAM Plan by instituting a compulsory uniform format for all company annual reports which have to be submitted to the Inland Revenue and the Department of Statistics. This is embodied in a document known as the 'Déclaration Statistique et Fiscale' (DSF), or Statistical and Fiscal Declaration.

The systematic classification of goods and services is well established in industrial economics, where it is intended to facilitate research and the analysis of market structure. By linking root codes in the main accounting framework with the SIC, wide-ranging disaggregated information on the operations of large, diversified companies and conglomerates would be generated. For each item, the first two/three digits (root codes) are those specified in the main accounting framework of the Plan listed earlier here. The other digits include those specified in the SIC which are applicable to the item in question. The Standard Industrial Classification adopted by OCAM is based on the Brussels Trade Nomenclature (BTN) for goods and the International Standard Industrial Classification (ISIC) in respect of services. This yields 65 groupings as shown in Appendix 1.

The ISIC digits are combined with those of the main accounting framework in order to specify a given item of segmental information. For example, a logging company may use the classification code 7114448 for line of business and geographical sales of one of its products thus:

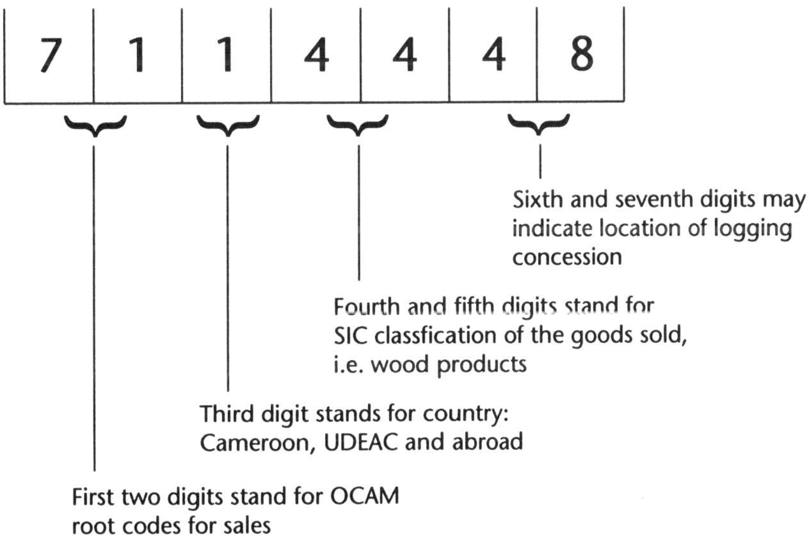

The nomenclature system and rules for data classification are contained in the DSF framework.[1] For example, Figure 3.1 shows a flow chart for the classification of concrete iron and explains the linkage between OCAM Plan classifications and entries in the DSF format.

1 Model DSF tables can be obtained from the Permanent Secretary for the OCAM Accounting Plan, Department of Statistics, Ministry of Economy and Planning, Yaoundé, Cameroon.

Figure 3.1 Flow chart for classification of concrete iron

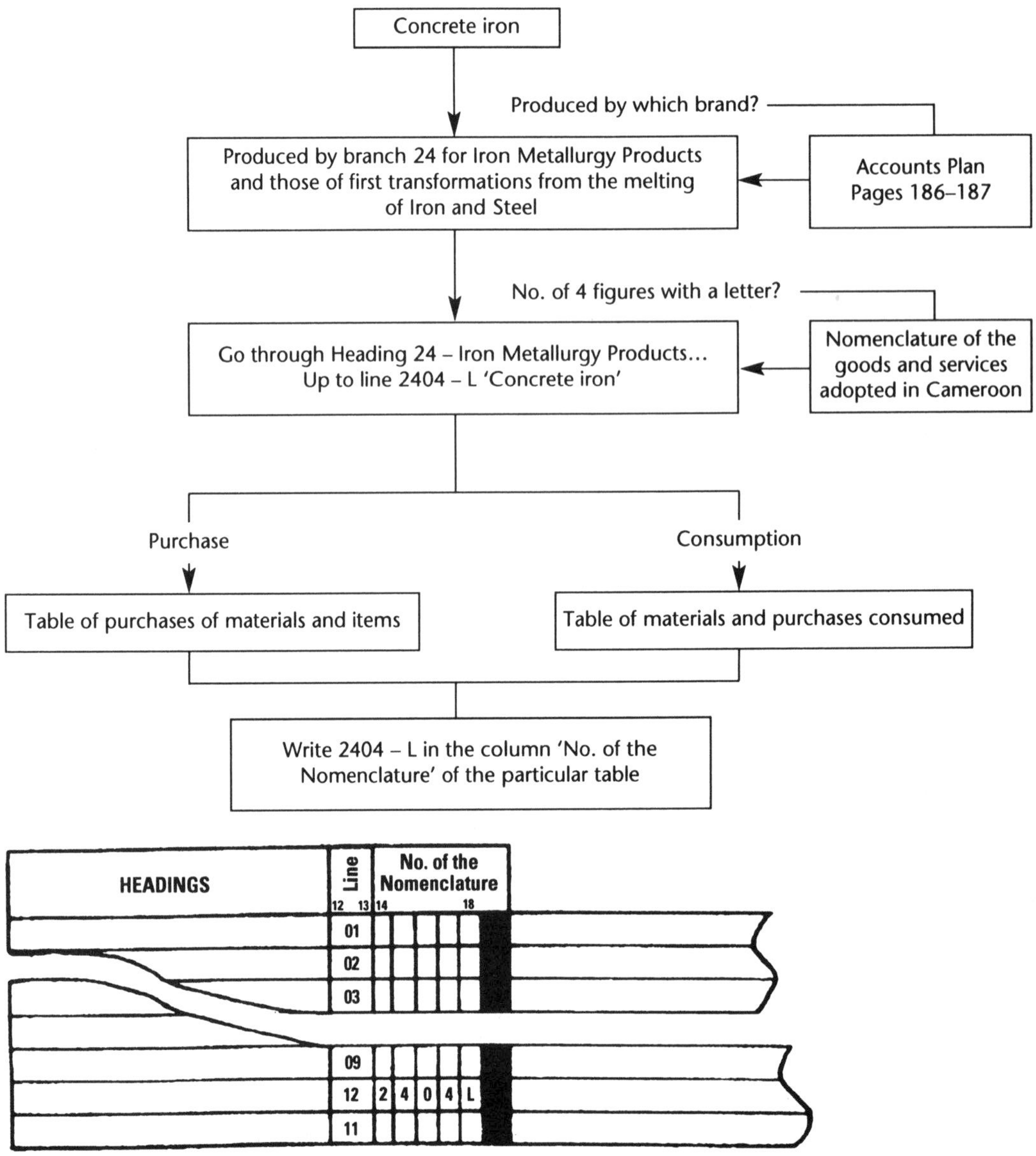

A few examples of DSF tables are shown in Appendices 2–9. It is important to note that the full document contains over fifty such tables, encompassing hundreds of mandatory items with wide-ranging segmental data by geographical area and line of business.

Small companies are exempted from submitting the DSF report. Medium-sized companies are required to submit an abridged or simplified version with fewer disclosures. However, all large companies are required to submit the full DSF report. The DSF report is generally divided into five sections (see a few extracts in Appendices 2–9). The tables are ingeniously structured in a manner which leads to the extrapolation of wide-ranging segmental information by line of business and geographical area in conformity with the ISIC and the BTN.

The tables in the first section deal with general information about the nature and structure of the company such as its main activities, distribution of share ownership, main business segments and their geographical locations, turnover, investments, number of employees and so on. The second section is concerned with the main financial statements, namely a modular income statement incorporating separate sections for gross profit and value added, a source and application of funds statement and the balance sheet. The other three sections contain further disaggregated information related to the main financial statements. Taken overall, the extent of disclosure required by this document considerably exceeds that of the OECD guidelines and closely matches the more extensive United Nations proposals (Forrester, 1983; Elad, 1996, 1998).

3.3 Forest resource management and OCAM accounting

One interesting feature of OCAM principles is the requirement that a wide range of externalities be 'internalised' in terms of various taxes shown in Appendix 7: e.g. council tax (line 03), forest tax (line 09) and so on. Council tax is payable to the relevant local authority and can be seen as partial compensation to the local community or to society for some of the adverse environmental effects of a company's operations. The local authority is in turn expected to provide services to the community: sanitation, street lighting, road maintenance, sewerage, infrastructure, and so forth. Similarly, the forest tax paid by logging companies is intended to finance a parastatal organisation known as the *Office National de Développement des Forêts* (ONADEF) which takes care of forest regeneration and management, thereby providing at least some (though not total) compensation to society for the adverse environmental effects of the operations of forest exploitation companies. The way in which the revenue derived from forest taxes is allocated to stakeholders will be explained in Chapter 4.

The link between OCAM segmental disclosures and the Standard Industrial Classification in this context is instructive. For example, code 02 in Appendix 1 requires companies to indicate the amount of silvicultural and forestry products extracted in volume and monetary terms. Similarly, code 01 relates to animal breeding and wildlife, while other codes cover metals, chemicals and mineral resources. National statisticians collate this data (in both quantity/volume and monetary terms) for the entire country in order to give policy-makers an indication of the rate of depletion of natural resources which can be attributed to the operations of large transnational corporations, or indigenous enterprises, on geographical and/or sectoral bases. This information is also vital for assessment of sustainable economic development.

In the case of forest resources, the OCAM Plan provides a comprehensive classification framework based upon code 44 in Appendix 1. This root code is expanded to cover every conceivable species of local tree and the appropriate tax rate per m^3 that is applicable to each of the three geographical segments which constitute Cameroon's forest belt (see Appendix 10). These tax rates are derived from the FOB (free on board) export price of each species, which is adjusted to compensate for transport costs. For example, Zone 3 has the lowest values (implying lower taxes to compensate for transport costs) because it is far away from the seaport. These matters will be explained in detail in the next chapter.

In addition to taxation, the OCAM classification model is used to support sustainable forest management. For example, Appendix 11 shows how it is incorporated into tables that specify the minimum diameter that each species must attain before it can be harvested in a sustainable manner if other aspects of sustainable forestry have been taken care of.

The OCAM Plan has also been used to support macroeconomic planning, fiscal policy decision-making, performance evaluation and supervision of the activities of large transnational companies by the state. In particular, there is a unique linkage between the accounting disclosures generated by the Plan and a package of incentives granted in conformity with the Investment Code, e.g. tax concessions, exemption from import duties over a specified period, exemption from taxes on profits, and, in the case of timber and mining companies, from the payment of royalties over several years (SEEC, 1988).

The factors which are considered for granting these incentives are accounting and financial disclosures generated by the OCAM Plan such as:

- The level of value added generated by the company;
- Number of local employees;
- Vocational training of employees;
- Use of local raw materials;
- Contribution to domestic capital formation;
- Location of operations in areas with inadequate infrastructure;
- High level of investment;
- Job creation programmes or potential, and so on.[2]

The package of incentives granted to companies on the basis of accounting and corporate social disclosures in conformity with the 1960 Investment Code[3] can be classified into four categories as shown in Table 3.1.

---

2 It is important to note that these items cover all the accounting information needs of developing countries identified by Briston (1984) and Wallace (1988). They include, *inter alia*, information necessary for assessment of: contribution to capital formation, foreign exchange reserves, transfer of technology, training of local people, local equity participation, value added, employment, investments on both sectoral and geographical bases.

3 It is important to note that this Investment Code was revised in the late 1980s and in 1994.

Table 3.1 Cameroon Investment Code (1960)

• Preferential Treatment A: allows duty-free entry of the required raw materials and capital goods for over ten years and grants exemption from indirect taxes for a period of up to three years, including exemption from new taxes and changes in rates of existing ones.
• Preferential Treatment B: the enterprise may be eligible to obtain, in addition to the benefits of preferential Treatment A, exemption for a period of up to five years from taxes on profits and, in the case of mining and forestry, from the payment of royalties. They are also eligible for any benefits from new tax laws which might be introduced during the first ten years of their operations.
• Preferential Treatment C: large enterprises may conclude an agreement with the government under which they may receive all or part of the privileges of Preferential Treatment B. The agreement in each case will also define other government guarantees.
• Preferential Treatment D: applies to enterprises making an investment of particular importance to the long-term economic development of the country. It grants all the benefits of preferential treatment C as well as a guarantee that new taxes and tax rates will not apply to such enterprises for up to 25 years.

(*Source:* Adapted from Ndongko (1975, p.113))

These disclosures should appear in a corporate report audited by a UDEAC-approved accountant and form the basis for a decision on the type of investment incentive to be granted (Letenou, 1988; SEEC, 1988). At first sight, it would appear that accounting has effectively been used here as a tool for promoting economic planning and development policy. However, this arrangement has instead helped to rationalise the expropriation of natural resources by foreign multinationals. This is largely due to the fact that there are few indigenous enterprises which can generate 'impressive' financial indicators approaching the threshold required for claiming the incentives. As Ndongko (1986, p.104) puts it:

> One of the effects of this legislation [the Investment Code] has been the low contribution by nationals to the formation of capital of industrial enterprises ... whereas these [foreign] firms import machinery on a tax-free basis the same privilege is refused the Cameroonian businessmen.

Furthermore, in the case of logging companies, the significant tax concessions which are granted in conformity with the Investment Code seem to betray the whole spirit of 'internalisation of externalities' via taxation which the OCAM conceptual framework implicitly advocates. Thankfully, this generous package of tax incentives was whittled down substantially by subsequent fiscal reforms in 1994 (see, for example, Nzakou, 1995).

3.4 Conclusion

The foregoing discussion suggests that, unlike conventional accounting or IASC pronouncements, the OCAM Plan satisfies most of the disclosure recommendations of the literature on accounting in developing countries (e.g. Enthoven, 1977; Briston,

1978, 1984; Samuels and Oliga, 1982; Wallace, 1988; Samuels, 1990). As Forrester (1983, p. 37) put it:

> The French accounting systems, which have been so widely introduced in the 1970s, prescribe very full disclosure, and the use of business accounts for national statistics and planning. British-style accounts, since the Cohen commission of 1945, have not had such aims; and thus Nigerians and Ghanaians have been taught to think differently. Now they seek to understand their neighbours.

3.5 Summary of key points

- The OCAM PCG is a forerunner of the 1982 French *Plan Comptable Général.* It is the first ever *plan comptable* that included Anglo-Saxon issues such as requirements for consolidation, the compulsory inclusion of notes to the accounts, and the disclosure of accounting policies. These innovations were subsequently incorporated into the 1982 French *plan comptable* as a result of the EU Fourth Directive.
- The OCAM PCG prescribes very extensive disclosure requirements based upon the Brussels Trade Nomenclature and the International Standard Industrial Classification. These disclosure requirements cover all the accounting information needs of developing countries identified by Briston (1984) and Wallace (1988). They include, *inter alia,* information necessary for the assessment of: contribution to capital formation, foreign exchange reserves, transfer of technology, training of local people, local equity participation, value added, employment, natural resources, and investments on both sectoral and geographical bases.
- OCAM-based disclosures are used to support environmental management, macroeconomic planning, and fiscal policy decision-making.
- The framework of the OCAM PCG incorporates extensive natural resource accounting information relating to minerals, chemicals, metals, livestock, wildlife, forests, etc. in volume and in monetary terms. The collation of this information on geographical and sectoral bases by national statisticians can give government officials an indication of the rate of depletion of natural resources which can be attributed to the operations of large multinational companies.

References

Beeny, J H (1976), *European Financial Reporting – France,* London, ICAEW.

Briston, R J (1978), 'The Evolution of Accounting in Developing Countries', *International Journal of Accounting Education and Research,* 14, pp. 105–20.

Briston, R J (1984), 'Accounting Standards and Host Country Control of Multinationals', *British Accounting Review,* 16, Spring, pp. 12–26.

Capelle, M (1986), 'Accounting Standards in France', in *Harmonisation of Accounting Standards: Achievements and Prospects,* Paris, OECD, pp. 52–6.

Elad, C M (1996), 'Implementing the OCAM Plan: Two Contrasting Case Studies', *Advances in International Accounting,* Vol. 9, pp. 47–72.

Elad, C M (1998), 'Corporate Disclosure Regulation and Practice in the Developing Countries of Central Africa', *Advances in Public Interest Accounting,* Vol. 7, pp. 51–106.

Emmanuel, C R and Gray, S J (1978), 'Segmental Disclosures by Multibusiness Multinational Companies: A Proposal', *Accounting and Business Research,* Vol. 8, pp. 169–77.

Enthoven, A J H (1977), *Accountancy Systems in Third World Economies,* Amsterdam, North-Holland Publishing.

Forrester, D A R (1983), 'Comment va-t-il in Africa: A Study of the Influence of French Accounting', *AUTA Review,* 15(2), Autumn, pp. 28–40.

Kinzonzi, M N K (1984), *Normalisation Comptable: Facteur d'Accélération du Développement Economique,* Paris, Foucher.

Letenou, E. (1988), 'Comment solliciter un agrément au code des investissements', *Le Reflet,* Douala, Cameroon Chamber of Commerce, April/May, pp. 26–9.

Ndongko, W (1975), *Planning for Economic Development in a Federal State: The Case of Cameroon, 1960-1971,* Weltforum Verlag Museum, Germany.

Ndongko, W (1986), 'The Political Economy of Development in Cameroon: Relations between the State, Indigenous Business and Foreign Investors', in M Schatzberg and I W Zartman (eds), *The Political Economy of Cameroon,* Connecticut, Praeger, pp. 83–110.

Nzakou, A (1995), *Comptabilité et Réforme Fiscalo-Douanière,* Douala, ESSEC.

Revue Française de Comptabilité (1988), 'La Troisième Edition du Plan Comptable de L'OCAM', *Revue Française de Comptabilité,* October, 194, 17–18.

Samuels, J M (1990), 'Accounting for Development: An Alternative Approach', in R S O Wallace, J M Samuels and R J Briston (eds), *Research in Third World Accounting,* London, JAI Press, 1(1), pp. 67–86.

Samuels, J M and Oliga, J C (1982), 'Accounting Standards in Developing Countries', *International Journal of Accounting Education and Research,* 18, pp. 69–88.

Service d'Etudes Economiques du Cameroun (1988), *Répertoire des Industries et Activités de la République du Cameroun et Code des Investissements,* Douala, SEEC.

Wallace, R S O (1988), 'Intranational and International Consensus on the Importance of Disclosure Items in Financial Reports: A Nigerian Case Study', *British Accounting Review,* 20, pp. 223–65.

4

Forestry Policy and Taxation

This chapter presents a concise review and appraisal of the fiscal aspects of Cameroon's forestry policy over the period 1994–8. It will be shown here that a number of sweeping reforms that were introduced within the World Bank's market-oriented structural adjustment programme have resulted in: (i) a dramatic increase in forest tax revenue, (ii) policies that are designed to protect the traditional rights of local communities living in areas under logging exploitation, (iii) a more participatory approach to forest management involving major stakeholders, and (iv) policies that are designed to ensure that more sustainable forest management practices are adopted.

The forest taxes discussed in this chapter fall largely within line 09 of the framework of the OCAM Plan in Appendix 7. They do not include normal taxation for companies (e.g. corporation tax or VAT). A description of different categories of forest is given in the next section in order to set the scene for subsequent analysis of the system of forestry taxation in Cameroon.

4.1 Classification of forests

Article 20 of Cameroon's Forestry Law No. 94/01 classifies the national forest estate into two main categories (see Figure 4.1), namely: permanent forests (i.e. areas of land that are used only for forestry or as wildlife habitat) and non-permanent forests (i.e. areas that can be used for purposes other than forestry).

The permanent forest estate comprises:

(i) *State forests:* areas that are protected for wildlife and forest reserves intended for production, recreation, or preservation of the national biological heritage.

(ii) *Council forests:* forestlands that form part of the private property of a local authority.

Non-permanent forests comprise:

(i) *Private forests:* these are forestlands that belong to individuals and corporate bodies.

(ii) *Communal forests:* these are unclassified forests – they do not include orchards, agricultural plantations, fallow lands, and wooded land adjoining agricultural farms or pastoral facilities.

(iii) *Community forests:* this category forms part of the communal forest that is subject to a management agreement between a local community and the Ministry of the Environment and Forests.

Figure 4.1 Types of forest

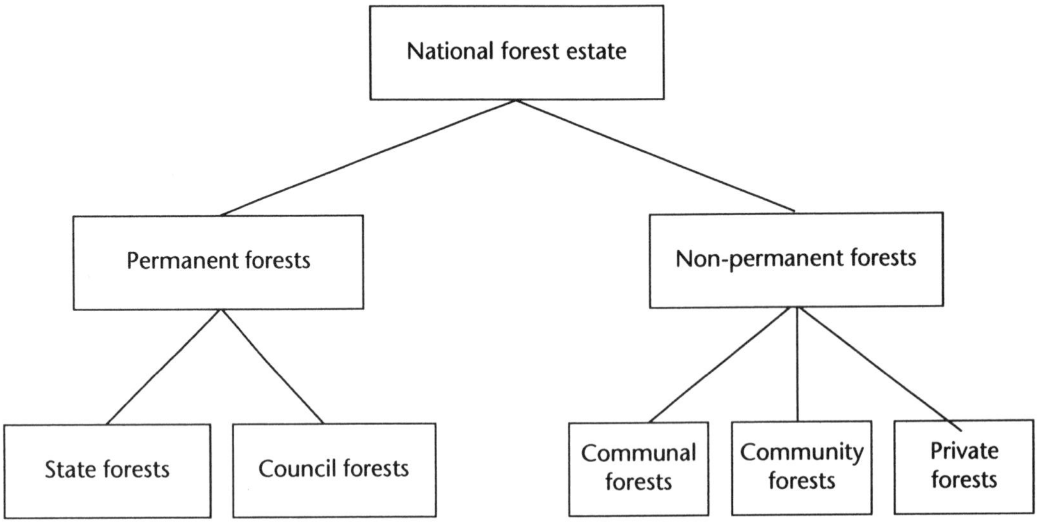

In order to analyse the complex system of forestry taxation in Cameroon, it is important to appreciate the type of exploitation permit required for each category of forest as set out in Table 4.1.

The columns in Table 4.1 show the main categories of forest, while the type of exploitation permit required for each type of forest is indicated by an asterisk in the relevant row. For example, only state forests can be exploited under an exploitation contract or a logging concession. Other types of exploitation permit include sale of 'standing volumes' (i.e. small areas within a concession); exploitation permit for scientific or medicinal purposes; and recuperation authorisation in the case of deforestation arising from road construction or other civil engineering projects. There are no asterisks in the 'Private Forest' column because exploitation permits are not required for logging operations in private forests.

Table 4.1 Forest exploitation permits

Type of permit \ Category of forest	State forest	Council forest	Communal forest	Community forest	Private forest
Exploitation contract (concessions)	•				
Sale of standing volume (small areas within a concession)	•	•	•	•	
Exploitation under state management	•	•		•	
Exploitation permit (a) Timber		•	•	•	
(b) Fuelwood/poles		•	•	•	
(c) Special products		•	•	•	
(d) Scientific purposes	•	•	•	•	
Individual felling authorisation		•	•	•	
Recuperation authorisation	•	•	•	•	

• = Type of permit required

(*Source:* Mount Cameroon Project (1995, p. 22))

4.2 Forestry taxation

Generally speaking, forest taxes in Cameroon can be classified into four major categories.

- **Area tax** ***(redevance forestière)***
  The area tax applies to the surface area within a logging concession. For example, during the period 1981–95, the area tax rate set by the government was 98 CFA francs (about 10 pence) per hectare per year. However, it will be explained later in this chapter that the 1997 Finance Law introduced a market-determined bidding mechanism whereby logging concessions are allocated to concessionaires who offer to pay the highest area tax rate per hectare. This means that the tax rates are now established by market forces rather than by state bureaucrats.

- **Stumpage tax** ***(taxe d'abattage)***
  The tax base for the stumpage fee depends on the value of the log and its zone of origin. The value of logs used in tax computations is specified in official tables published periodically by the government that cover every conceivable species of local tree (referred to as *valeurs mercuriales*). These tables also include different tax bases for three geographical segments which are intended to compensate for transport costs. Logs coming from zones which are closer to the seaport have a higher tax base than those coming from zones which are relatively far away from the port (see Appendix 10).

- **Export tax *(droits de sortie)***
  This is based on a flat rate (e.g. 25 per cent in 1996/97) imposed on the value of the log. In order to encourage a higher level of corporate value added in the forestry sector, the tax statutes require that processed wood (as opposed to unprocessed logs) be exempted from the export tax.

- **Progressive surtax on log export *(surtaxe progressive)***
  Currently, government regulations require that at least 70 per cent of the logs harvested by each company be processed by sawmills within the country. Otherwise, a progressive surtax will be imposed on unprocessed logs beyond the 30 per cent allowed, as shown in Table 4.2 below. The rationale behind this policy was the need to increase the local value added to timber and thereby stimulate industrialisation and employment opportunities in the domestic wood processing sector. Indeed, the perceived importance of this policy was manifested in a law adopted by Cameroon's National Assembly that sanctioned a complete log export ban with effect from April 1999.

4.3 Evolution of the forestry taxation system in Cameroon

4.3.1 Area tax and market-based allocation of concessions

Prior to a series of reforms in the mid-1990s which were inspired by the World Bank's structural adjustment programme, forest tax rates set by the government were very low and somewhat arbitrary. These taxes were not adjusted for inflation, and, as will be shown later, were surprisingly below the rates that potential concessionaires were able to pay. Furthermore, the tax system was characterised by low collection rates and a substantial erosion of the tax base through exemptions and tax concessions granted to powerful logging companies which actively lobby the policy-makers (see, for example, Vidal, 1990; Elad and Gray, 1991; Gauthier and Gersovitz, 1997).

For example, the area tax rate of 98 CFA francs per hectare per year remained unchanged throughout the period 1981–95 despite high rates of inflation and a 50 per cent devaluation of the CFA franc in 1994 which, taken together, made Cameroon's forest resources severely undertaxed. However, following an acute economic crisis in the late 1980s, the World Bank recommended a package of radical reforms within its structural adjustment programme which covered three main issues, namely: (i) transparency in allocation of forestry concessions through a market bidding mechanism; (ii) sustainability of logging operations through a requirement that forest management plans be established for all concessions; and (iii) a very substantial increase in all forest taxes.

These fiscal reforms were incorporated into the Forestry Code of 1994/95 which introduced a market-determined bidding mechanism whereby concessions are allocated to applicants who offer to pay the highest annual area tax rate per hectare of the concession. Following the implementation of this transparent auction system in 1995, it became evident that many logging companies were offering between 1,000

CFA francs and 4,000 CFA francs per hectare per year for small, short-term concessions (referred to as 'standing volumes'). This means that the area tax rate of 98 CFA francs per hectare per year applicable over the period 1991–5 was far less than 10 per cent of the rate that the logging companies were able to pay. As a result of this experience, the government increased the minimum floor level of the area tax that can be used as a basis for bidding for concessions from 98 CFA francs per hectare per year in 1994/95 to 300 CFA francs over 1995/96–1996/97, and to 1,500 francs in 1997/98. It was envisaged that the new area tax rates would be adjusted annually for inflation.

However, in view of the fact that periods of about 20 years are necessary for the implementation of any viable sustainable forest management plan, the 1994 Forestry Code included a requirement that all short-term concessions and licences be phased out. Accordingly, this law specifically forbids the renewal of existing licences at the end of their five-year life. Thereafter, only large fifteen-year concessions of about 200,000 hectares were available for auction. Concessions were to be awarded for an interim period of three years during which concessionaires were expected to meet the following conditions prior to firm confirmation of an offer:

- Development of forest management plans to be monitored and approved by the Ministry of Forests and the Environment.
- Establishment of a forest inventory.
- Establishment of a sawmill.
- Logging operations during the interim period were restricted to 2,500 hectares per year.

If the authorities are satisfied that a concessionaire has complied with the above criteria, a permanent logging permit is issued and the company is then able to log more intensively within its concession in conformity with the agreed forest management plan. The area tax rate payable during the interim period is 1,500 CFA francs per hectare per year. After the interim period, the tax rate is raised automatically to the level offered by the concessionaire in the bidding process. An annual inflation coefficient is applied to this rate to ensure that it retains its value in real terms.

4.3.2 Tax base for stumpage fee and export taxes

The arbitrary rates published periodically by the government as a basis for calculating stumpage fees and export taxes, referred to as *valeurs mercuriales,* resulted in severe undertaxation of the resource. In line with the market-oriented reform of the area tax, the 1997/98 Finance Law instituted the use of FOB (i.e. free on board) prices as the tax base for calculating stumpage fees for logs and processed wood, as shown in Table 4.2. This new tax base resulted in a dramatic increase in tax revenues (see Table 4.3), particularly in view of the fact that, on average, the old *valeurs mercuriales* were barely 15 per cent of the FOB price of processed wood, and 70 per cent of the FOB price of logs.

Table 4.2 Evolution of forestry taxation in Cameroon

	1994/95	1995/96	1996/97	1997/98
Area tax	98 CFA Frs	300 CFA Frs	300 CFA Frs	1,500 CFA Frs
	/ha/ year	/ha/ year	/ha/ year	/ha/ year
Tax base for export tax and stumpage tax	*Valeur mercuriale*	*Valeur mercuriale*	*Valeur mercuriale*	FOB export price
Export tax rates:				
Logs	25%	25%	25%	17.5%
Sawn wood	15%	20%	20%	12.5%
Second transformation	15%	15%	15%	12.5%
Stumpage tax rate	5%	7%	2.5%	2.5%
Progressive surtax on log exports beyond the 30% allowed by law	25%	31–45%: 5,000Frs/m^3 45–60%: 7,500Frs/m^3 >60%: 10,000Frs/m^3	31–45%: 8,000Frs/m^3 41–50%: 10,500Frs/m^3 >50%: 15,000Frs/m^3	31–40%: 8,000Frs/m^3 41–50%: 10,000Frs/m^3 >50%: 15,000Frs/m^3

However, in 1997, the logging companies complained that the new forest tax statutes were too harsh and could threaten their operations in the country. Following a series of meetings and consultations involving representatives of the timber trade and the government, an agreement was reached with the logging companies which effectively reduced the new tax rates. The government was particularly concerned that the reforms could trigger a high rate of tax evasion. The main changes announced in the 1997/98 Finance Law were:

- The area tax will apply only to 'useful' areas within the concession.
- Elimination of the export surtax on 'promotional' species (as defined in Appendix 10).
- 25 per cent reduction in FOB values used in calculating export taxes on processed wood.
- 15 per cent reduction in FOB values used in calculating the stumpage tax and log export taxes.

Table 4.3 Forest tax revenues

	1992/93	1993/94	1994/95	1995/96	1996/97
Production volume ('000 m³)	1809	2430	2520	2803	3500
Export volume ('000 m³)	1680	1764	1950	2300	2900
Export value (billions of CFA francs)	54	89	91	91	126
Forest tax revenue (billions of CFA francs)	1.5	8.7	20.6	21.0	24.5
Forestry export taxes/ forestry exports	0.3	7.4	20.2	18.5	15.2
Share of GDP (%)	4.3	8.0	8.5	9.1	8.9

(*Source:* Cameroonian authorities and IMF estimates)

4.4 Evaluation of forestry policy and taxation

In this chapter, it has been made evident that, prior to the mid-1990s, logging companies operating in Cameroon benefited from very low taxation. This problem was, to a large extent, reversed by the reforms introduced in the 1997/98 Finance Law which relied largely on the discipline of market forces. For example, FOB prices became the new tax base for stumpage fees and export taxes, and a market-determined bidding mechanism was used to allocate logging concessions to applicants who offered to pay the highest area tax per hectare per year. As a result of these reforms, forest tax revenues rose dramatically from 8.7 billion CFA francs in 1993/94 to 21 billion CFA francs in 1995/96 for broadly similar production volumes, as shown in Table 4.3.

The new regulations transfer some of the responsibility for sustainable forest management from government departments to concessionaires (e.g. establishment of management plans, forest inventories etc.), leaving government officials to concentrate on monitoring compliance with the provisions of the Forestry Code.

Another major advantage of the fiscal reforms relates to the notion of value added. For instance, forest companies that export processed wood and thereby generate high levels of local value added (compared with companies that export raw logs) enjoy substantial tax concessions. The emphasis on value added can also be seen in terms of the 1997 Finance Law, which clearly specifies the way in which the area tax revenue is allocated to the state, communes (or local councils) and communities (or people who live near logging sites) as follows:

- State 50 per cent of area tax revenue.
- Communes 40 per cent of area tax revenue.
- Communities 10 per cent of area tax revenue.

Before this law came into force, there were unwritten rules which governed some of the informal arrangements and strategies used by logging companies to appease local communities (referred to as *parafiscalité*) in order to facilitate their operations. For example, many logging companies paid 1000 CFA francs per cubic metre of timber to communities around the logging site, although there was absolutely no legal basis for such payment.

Similarly, some logging companies were required to construct roads, health centres, education facilities or other amenities requested by local communities. However, the 1997 Finance Law effectively eliminated the need for such informal arrangements *(parafiscalité)* by spelling out the proportion of the area tax that should be allocated to each social constituency, thereby alleviating some eco-justice problems. The proportion of the area tax revenue allocated to the state (i.e. 50 per cent) was intended to finance a parastatal organisation known as the *Office National de Developpement des Forêts* (ONADEF), which supposedly takes care of forest regeneration and management.

4.5 Summary of key points

The main advantages and disadvantages of Cameroon's new forestry policy reviewed in this chapter can be summarised thus:

Advantages of the new forestry policy

- The use of FOB prices as the new tax base for stumpage fees and export taxes, and the adoption of a market-determined bidding mechanism for establishing area tax rates, have resulted in a very substantial increase in tax revenue.
- The new forest tax statutes seek to resolve some social justice problems by spelling out the modalities for the allocation of area tax revenue to stakeholders – i.e. state, communes (or municipalities) and local communities.
- Strong emphasis on the notion of value added on timber is intended to stimulate the development of the local wood industry and employment in the sector.
- A market-based system for the auction of logging concessions supports sustainable forest management because the prerequisites for submitting bids include a requirement that appropriate forest management plans be established.
- The use of FOB prices in determining stumpage fees and export taxes along with the market-based bidding mechanism for establishing area tax rates offers:
  - (i) Very little leeway for manipulation of the tax base by government officials;
  - (ii) Transparency/objectivity;
  - (iii) Safeguards against corruption;
  - (iv) The efficient allocation of resources, since the companies that win logging concessions are those that value them highly, as evidenced by their willingness to pay the highest area tax rate per hectare.

Disadvantages of the new forestry policy

- A lack of capacity/resources for monitoring compliance.
- Civil servants may not like to see some of their functions internalised within logging companies. Hence, although well-intentioned, the market-oriented reforms may not effectively reduce rent seeking.
- Responsibility for the collection of forest taxes is assigned to different bodies: for instance, the Forestry Department collects area tax and stumpage fees, and the Customs Department collects export taxes, whereas the Inland Revenue is not directly involved. A lack of effective co-ordination of these responsibilities makes it difficult to monitor tax-evasion problems.
- Transfer pricing problems make it difficult to ascertain the accuracy of segmental data used in forest tax calculations in conformity with the model outlined in Appendix 10.

References

Elad, C M and Gray, S J (1991), 'Value Added Accounting in Equatorial Africa', Paper presented at the 1991 Congress of the European Accounting Association, Maastricht, The Netherlands.

Gauthier, B and Gersovitz, M (1997), 'Revenue Erosion through Exemption and Evasion in Cameroon', *Journal of Public Economics,* 64, pp. 407–24.

Mount Cameroon Project (1995), 'Report on a Seminar on the New Forestry Law in Cameroon', Buea, Cameroon.

Vidal, J (1990), 'New Gods in the Jungle – Cameroon Rainforests', *Guardian,* 2 March, p. 21.

5

Auditing in the Forestry Industry

5.1 Introduction

The need to monitor compliance with the far-reaching market-oriented reform of forest tax statutes in Cameroon analysed in Chapter 4 poses major challenges for tax inspectors, auditors, company accountants, foresters and national statisticians. For example, left to their own devices, logging companies could actively use transfer pricing techniques to distort geographical segment data in order to minimise their stumpage fees and export taxes. Furthermore, the potential for substantial revenue erosion through the underdeclaration of production volume, or through deliberate manipulation of the OCAM classification scheme for logs and processed wood by unscrupulous forest managers and accountants, heightens the need for effective audit strategies.

In addition to auditing problems associated with the administration of forest tax statutes, a broad range of environmental auditing problems could also be identified from the perspectives of logging companies, government officials, environmental campaigners, representatives of indigenous people, consumers, and other social constituencies. A praiseworthy development in this regard is that, in recent years, sustained pressure from some of these stakeholders – notably 'green' consumers and international agencies such as the World Bank and the European Union – has prompted several logging companies in the Congo basin rainforest to adopt forest management audit and ecolabelling schemes.

This chapter examines the role and impact of consumer-driven environmental audit and ecolabelling strategies which have evolved in the forestry sector by using a case study of Leroy Gabon, a large Franco-German logging concession in the Congo basin rainforest. Although the case study relates to Gabon, all logging concessions in Cameroon and other countries that form part of the Congo basin rainforest are under similar regulatory pressures (see, for example, Eba'a Atyi, 1997). Another key feature of this chapter is that it locates the institutional mechanisms for forest stewardship audit within the New Public Management agenda, and thus sets the scene for an analysis of the tensions that arise between the claims to professionalism of forest auditors and the sustainability concerns of stakeholders.

The material presented here is in three main parts. The first part reviews the development of auditing standards by the Forest Stewardship Council (FSC). The FSC is an independent, non-profit, international non-governmental organisation founded in 1993 to: (i) develop auditing standards that are designed to ensure that the world's forests are well managed and (ii) accredit auditors who certify the quality of forest management. The second part of the chapter analyses the impact of FSC auditing standards on corporate governance using a case study of Leroy Gabon, while the third part considers some attendant theoretical issues.

5.2 The development of auditing standards in the forestry sector

In response to pressures from 'green' consumers, and growing scepticism among other stakeholders regarding environmental claims made by companies (see, e.g., WWF, 1994), a number of forest auditing and certification schemes have evolved which take three basic forms: (i) first-party audit refers to an internal assessment by a company of its own systems and practices; (ii) second-party audit is an assessment of a company's system and practices by a customer or trade association; and (iii) third-party audits involve an onsite assessment by a neutral organisation based upon a set of accepted standards (Hansen, 1997, p.17).

Many third-party forest auditors also issue ecolabels that serve as a tool to communicate to consumers that wood products come from 'well-managed' forests. The focus in this paper will be on third-party audit, since this is the most credible and objective of the three approaches. Generally speaking, such audits can be described as either systems-based (e.g. the Canadian Standards Association's Sustainable Forest Management Standards) or performance-based (e.g. auditing standards issued by the Forest Stewardship Council). In a systems-based model, a third-party auditor is called in to establish whether or not a company's environmental management system meets the goals that it was designed to attain. By contrast, in the performance-based model, the forest auditor is mainly required to determine the extent to which the auditee has complied with a set of previously agreed performance measures.

5.3 The Forest Stewardship Council

In the late 1980s, increased consumer awareness and public concern about the degradation and destruction of the world's forests triggered a proliferation of dubious ecolabels and misleading claims regarding 'sustainability' within the timber trade. For example, an authoritative study by the Worldwide Fund for Nature (WWF, 1994, p. 2) indicated that, out of a sample of 80 different environmental claims found on wood and paper products, only three could even be partially substantiated.

In view of the need to remedy such problems, the Forest Stewardship Council was established in 1993 as an all-encompassing private-sector body for accrediting third-party forest auditors. It was founded by a diverse group of representatives from environmental institutions, the timber trade, indigenous peoples' organisations, academia, and several NGOs, from 25 countries. According to its mission statement, the FSC seeks to promote good forest management throughout the world, based on a set of principles designed to ensure that forests of all types are managed in ways that are environmentally appropriate, socially beneficial and economically viable (WWF,

1994, p. 12). The FSC planned to achieve these goals by establishing auditing standards and by evaluating and accrediting forest management auditors worldwide (Hansen, 1997, p. 20).

In 1994, the FSC embarked on a two-year consultative process, involving large-scale questionnaire surveys and interviews carried out in several countries around the world, which led to the establishment of nine principles and criteria for sustainable forest management applicable to natural forests (temperate, tropical, or boreal) and plantations as summarised in Table 5.1. Representatives of social constituencies such as governments, industry, forest owners and managers, academia, environmental campaigners and indigenous NGOs were involved in the consultative process (WWF 1994, p. 12; Upton and Bass, 1996).

Table 5.1 Summary of the Forest Stewardship Council principles and criteria

- **Principle 1: Compliance with laws and FSC principles**
  Forest management shall respect all applicable laws of the country in which they occur and international treaties and agreements to which the country is signatory, and comply with all FSC principles and criteria.
- **Principle 2: Tenure and use rights and responsibilities**
  Long-term tenure and use rights to land and forest resources shall be clearly defined, documented and legally established.
- **Principle 3: Indigenous peoples' rights**
  The legal and customary rights of indigenous peoples to own, use and manage their lands, territories and resources shall be recognised and respected.
- **Principle 4: Community relations and workers' rights**
  Forest management operations shall maintain or enhance the long-term social economic well-being of forest workers and local communities.
- **Principle 5: Benefits from the forest**
  Forest management operations shall encourage the optimal and efficient use of the forest's multiple products and services, in order to ensure economic viability and a wide range of environmental, social and economic benefits.
- **Principle 6: Environmental impact**
  Forest management operations shall maintain the critical ecological functions of the forest and minimise adverse impacts on biological diversity, water resources, soils, non-timber resources, and unique and fragile ecosystems and landscapes.
- **Principle 7: Management plan**
  A management plan consistent with FSC principles and appropriate to the scale of the operations shall be written, implemented and kept up to date, clearly stating the objectives of management and the means of achieving them.
- **Principle 8: Monitoring and assessment**
  Regular monitoring should be conducted that assesses the condition of the forest, yields of forest products, chain of custody, and management operations and their social and environmental impacts.
- **Principle 9: Relations between natural forests and plantations**
  Primary forests, well-developed secondary forests, and sites of major environmental, social or cultural significance shall be conserved. Such areas shall not be replaced by tree plantations or other land uses.

The broad, ambitious and very demanding nature of the nine principles and criteria summarised in Table 5.1 can be explained in terms of the need to accommodate the requirements of all stakeholders in order to achieve a consensus. However, since FSC-based audits are voluntary, compliance with its principles and criteria will largely depend on the influence of market forces and the ability of dominant stakeholders such as environmental activist organisations (notably Friends of the Earth, WWF, Rainforest Coalition) and 'green' consumers to exert pressure on forest companies. This point ties in well with the argument of stakeholder theorists that, as the level of a stakeholder's power increases, the importance of meeting that stakeholder's needs also increases (see, e.g., Roberts, 1998, p. 228).

In the case of Leroy Gabon, a Franco-German logging concession in the Congo basin rainforest that will be analysed in detail later, Figure 5.1 illustrates some of the stakeholder pressures that compelled the company to have its forest management processes audited by an FSC-accredited auditor. The dominant stakeholders here are 'green' consumers in the European plywood market. This social constituency, represented in Figure 5.1 as 'Environmental Campaigners', have lobbied the European Union (EU) to promote the FSC agenda via the Lomé Convention, a protocol agreement on trade and development assistance between the EU and 46 African, Caribbean, and Pacific (ACP) countries. Thus the EU now sees FSC ecolabels as tantamount to sustainable forest management and has decided to fund the FSC's scheme, which is also backed by WWF (Kiekens, 1997, p. 23).

Figure 5.1 Influences on Forest Stewardship Auditing

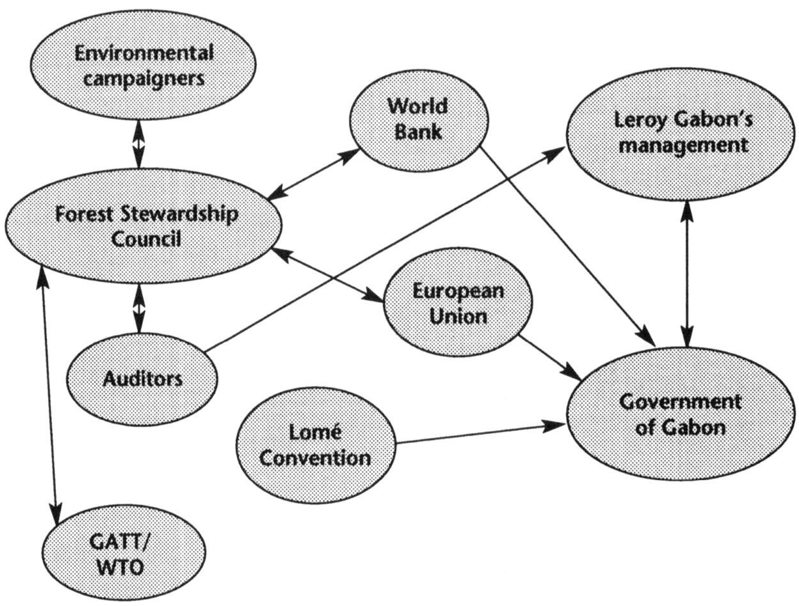

Furthermore, the World Bank has recently decided to support FSC audit certification of 100 million hectares of tropical forest by 2005. The following comment from the president of the World Bank at a press conference during the Earth Summit II (cited in Kiekens 1997, p. 23) bears out a strategic alliance between the EU, WWF, the World Bank and the FSC:

> As well, the Bank will assist in increasing the number of forests and plantations which are being used and managed under certification from the Forest Stewardship Council, an international professional organisation, from less than 1 per cent of potential land to more than 7 per cent.

However, as Kiekens (1997) notes, some interest groups (particularly a number of tropical timber producing countries) have challenged the *raison d'être* of FSC-based ecolabelling of timber, pointing out that it constitutes an impediment to free trade that may be contrary to the framework of the General Agreement on Tariffs and Trade (GATT), or that of its successor body, the World Trade Organisation (WTO).

In line with the position of stakeholder theorists that the power of a particular social constituency determines the importance of meeting the needs of that social constituency, 'green' consumers have formed powerful cartels or 'buying groups' of companies who want to compel logging companies to comply with FSC principles. These buying groups are committed to purchasing wood and wood products only from well-managed forests evidenced by a clean audit report and any of the FSC-backed ecolabels. The most prominent buying group is the WWF 95 Club that includes companies which agreed, in 1991, to phase out the purchase of wood products from non-certified sources by 1995 (see WWF, 1994, p. 18).

In order to maintain their group membership, the companies are expected to submit progress reports to WWF every six months, and to designate a senior manager who is charged with the implementation of buying group policies. Founding members of the WWF 95 Club include some of the largest UK retailers of 'do-it-yourself' materials, wholesalers, and distributors such as B&Q, MFI, Homebase and Boots (among many others).

Membership of the WWF 95 Club rose from 24 to 47 by the end of 1995, representing 2,200 suppliers and 56,000 lines of product, with a turnover of £2.7 billion (WWF, 1996). However, given that it proved impossible for members to completely phase out uncertified wood products by the 1995 deadline, the group decided to adopt a new policy which merely requires members to increase the share of certified products in their supplies. Currently, there are 89 companies in the UK WWF 95 Club. It is noteworthy that there are similar WWF buyer cartels in some European countries: e.g. WWF Club 1997 in Belgium and Holland, and the WWF Club 1998 in Germany (Kiekens, 1997, p. 35).

This seemingly sporadic emergence of buyer cartels can actually be seen as part of an active strategic posture adopted by companies that feel threatened by the onslaught of pressures from environmental campaigners, in order to manage stakeholder social responsibility demands. This observation provides a practical illustration of some of the key arguments that were advanced at a conceptual level by stakeholder theorists such as Ullmann (1985) and Roberts (1998, p. 228). In the next section, the Leroy Gabon case study will be used to analyse the impact of a third-party audit of forest management processes based upon FSC principles.

5.4 Case study of Leroy Gabon

5.4.1 *Method*

In order to compile the case study, relevant information and supporting documents were secured from the following sources:

- The complete file containing photocopies of all key documents and correspondence relating to all protagonists in the Leroy Gabon affair (i.e. FSC, SGS, WWF, and Leroy Gabon), held at the head office of Friends of the Earth in London, was sent to the researcher at his request.
- Interviews with representatives of some of the major stakeholders such as forestry officers at the WWF regional office for Central Africa, and United Nations Development Programme officials working in the region.
- Internet postings at Web sites maintained by the FSC, SGS and the rainforest action network.
- Sundry articles on the Leroy Gabon affair in the local (i.e. Gabonese) press.

5.4.2 *Case study*

Leroy Gabon is a subsidiary company of Isoroy, a French company owned by a German conglomerate known as Glunz AG. Leroy's logging concession in Gabon is located at the heart of the Congo basin rainforest, which harbours a large diversity of flora and fauna including substantial populations of primates, elephants, and other large animals. According to Knight (1997), this forest ranks alongside those of the Amazon as some of the most biologically diverse in the world.

In response to consumer demands in the European plywood market, the company invited the Société Générale de Surveillance (SGS), an FSC-accredited auditor, to audit its forest management practices with a view to securing the right to use an ecolabel that would enhance marketability of its wood products. SGS audited Leroy's operations in La Forêt des Abeilles, an area of primary rainforest of extremely high biological value, and subsequently issued a certificate that would warrant Leroy Gabon to use an FSC-backed ecolabel. This move infuriated domestic stakeholders and also sparked off widespread outrage among environmental pressure groups and NGOs, which fiercely contested the issuance of the ecolabel.

The following passages from a communiqué entitled 'Good Intentions Betray Gabon Rainforest' that was issued by the Rainforest Action Network and published at the Web site: http://forests.org/gopher/africa/gabongoo.txt (dated 11 September 1997) encapsulate the key issues at stake here:

> An African rainforest that is home to scores of endangered species, including the rare lowland gorilla, is about to be logged mercilessly with the approval of the world's largest certifier of 'sustainable' timber.

> ... logging is about to begin with the blessing of an organisation that should be preventing it. The Forest Stewardship Council (FSC) was established in 1993 to help ensure the protection of the world's remaining primary forests through timber certification programmes. The FSC accredits auditors around the world, who in turn examine logging operations and determine if they can be called 'certified'. Principle 9 of the FSC guidelines indicates that to be considered 'certified', a logging operation must not destroy primary forest. Yet the FSC-approved certifier, SGS, has given Leroy the green light to log, even though much of the planned logging will take place in primary forest.
>
> The approval process for Leroy Gabon has been clouded by sloppy accounting and conflict of interests from the very beginning. Even though FSC rules require a certification programme to be independent from the rest of the forest industry, SGS has other divisions that stand to profit from contracts with governments and multinational corporations. Despite this, FSC Executive Director Tim Synnott dismissed international outrage over the certification, embracing the Leroy logging as 'good forest management'.

However, following intense lobbying and sustained pressure from campaigns launched by a number of environmental activist groups spearheaded by Friends of the Earth (UK) and Rettet den Regenwald (Germany), the FSC finally yielded. In an unprecedented development, the FSC certification (and thus ecolabel) awarded to Leroy Gabon was initially frozen, then subsequently defrozen, suspended, and finally revoked. These episodes in the Leroy Gabon case are now considered.

On 15 August 1996, Friends of the Earth (UK) and Rettet den Regenwald (Germany) wrote to Dr Tim Synott, Executive Director of the FSC, requesting that the certification of Leroy's operations in La Forêt des Abeilles by SGS be forestalled on the grounds that:

- The company is logging in primary rainforest of exceptionally high biological value (i.e. infringement of FSC Principle 9).
- The clean audit report and resultant certificate that SGS intended to issue will cover the company's proposed logging in a protected area known as the Lope Reserve which was illegal under Gabonese law (i.e. violation of FSC Principle 1).
- Lack of information on impact of the company's operations outside the Lope Reserve, where one scientific study had indicated an 80 per cent drop in chimpanzee populations in the five years since logging started (i.e. violation of FSC Principle 6 and Principle 8).

Friends of the Earth articulated these and other concerns in a number of protest letters and faxes to the FSC Executive Director from August 1996 to November 1996. In February 1997, five Gabonese NGOs pointed out in a series of press conferences and communiqués that the audit of Leroy's operations carried out by SGS manifested major infringements of FSC regulations (Kiekens, 1997, p. 19). These NGOs claimed that at least five of the nine FSC principles were glaringly violated. Accordingly, they went on to press for: (i) revocation of Leroy's audit certificate, and (ii) loss of accreditation of SGS from the FSC.

In response to these impassioned demands, the FSC Secretariat announced a freeze on Leroy's certification pending further investigations. Following these investigations, the Secretariat issued a document entitled 'FSC Evaluation of Complaints against SGS Forestry Certificate issued to Leroy Gabon' (hereafter, the Evaluation Report), which formed the basis for a subsequent ruling that Leroy's certification be defrozen. This new development incensed many stakeholders and environmental activist organisations which once again embarked on a fierce and well-co-ordinated protest (see, for example, Figure 5.2) which raged for several months until the FSC was finally compelled to revoke the certificate and provisionally suspend SGS.

Figure 5.2 Sample protest letter recommended by the Rainforest Action Network

Dear Ms Erwin

I am writing to express my dismay over the Forest Stewardship Council's approval of the Leroy logging concession in Gabon, an operation that independent agencies show will destroy primary forest. By allowing the certification of this cutting, FSC will be giving its blessing to a project that will imperil endangered species, including the lowland gorilla. Calling such a venture 'sustainable' lets deforestation pass as environmental action. The FSC should withdraw its support from Leroy in its current form.

I urge you to pass this information on to the FSC board, and to take a stand as FSC's US representative to end this wasteful, destructive venture.

Sincerely

(*Source:* Rainforest Action Network Web site)

The following environmental activist organisations and NGOs around the world vigorously denounced the Secretariat's Evaluation Report and called on the FSC board to decertify Leroy Gabon immediately:

Friends of the Earth (UK)
Rettet den Regenwald (Germany)
Greenpeace (Switzerland)
Reforest the Earth (UK)
CIAJE (Gabon)
Greenpeace International (Holland)
FERN (UK)
Rainforest Action Network (USA)
Environmental Defense Fund (USA)
Greenpeace (Germany)
Rainforest Information Centre (Australia)

On 21 July 1997, the above complainants criticised Leroy's certification on the following grounds in a joint protest letter addressed to FSC board members:

- *Violation of Principle 5 and Principle 7*
  These were acknowledged in the Secretariat's Evaluation Report thus:

  'The Secretariat supports the complainants' contention that the absence of a satisfactory management plan at the time of the evaluation was a violation of Principle 7, and this could have precluded the issue of a certificate' (Section 5.13.2.9 of the Evaluation Report).

  The Evaluation Report also concludes that Leroy's performance fell short of the standard spelled out in Principle 5. Accordingly, the complainants drew attention to the FSC's requirement that 'major failures in any individual principle would normally disqualify a candidate from certification or will lead to de-certification'.

- *Violation of Principle 9: Maintenance of natural forest*
  The Secretariat did not accept the complainants' charge that other principles were violated. In particular, there was considerable debate and disagreement within the FSC membership as to how Principle 9 should be interpreted. The complainants felt that it was ultimately the responsibility of the FSC board and General Assembly rather than the Secretariat or Executive Director to give guidance on controversial and far-reaching issues such as interpretation of Principle 9.

- *Violation of Principles 6 and 8: Environmental impact, monitoring and assessment*
  It is stated under Principle 6 that 'Environmental impacts shall be assessed prior to the commencement of site-disturbing operations.' The complainants contended that Leroy did not produce sufficient information on environmental impact. Furthermore, even the SGS conceded in its audit report that adequate data on the growth and the structure of the forest did not exist.

- *Part-certification*
  The certification granted by SGS to Leroy Gabon covered only two forest areas within their logging concession, namely Lot 28 and Lot 30. The complainants produced evidence that indicate that Leroy Gabon intended to harvest timber in all the lots within its concession – irrespective of whether or not these were certified – in order to achieve its desired cutting cycle. This means that the company had planned to carry out illegal logging in Lot 32, which is a designated reserve (Bayami, 1997, p. 3).

  However, SGS stated clearly on page 2 of its audit report that 'the forest management certificate for Lots 28 and 30 cannot be maintained if uncertified operations are undertaken outside these areas'. SGS also stated earlier on that page that, 'In addition, Leroy Gabon is harvesting in Lot 27.' This observation gave Friends of the Earth the necessary ammunition to argue that Leroy's certificate was invalid at the time it was issued and makes a mockery of the FSC requirement for total certification of all parts of a single operation.

- *Lack of independence and integrity*
  According to Friends of the Earth, the research station that produced much of the data that Leroy Gabon uses to justify its operations was supported by the company itself, and thus raises serious questions regarding its independence. Also, while the Leroy Gabon dispute was being considered by the FSC Board, a number of articles appeared in the *Financial Times* that reported the involvement of a senior executive of SGS in corruption scandals in Pakistan which were likely to undermine its integrity and independence (Hall, 1997). For instance, Hall, Bokhari and Burns (1997, p. 30) report:

> Société Générale de Surveillance, the Swiss testing and inspection company, has suspended a senior executive while it investigates allegations of corruption in its Pakistan operations linked to Benazir Bhutto. ... SGS is often used by governments of developing countries to help prevent capital flight, commercial fraud, and evasion of custom duties.

Second, an article in a Gabonese newspaper (*La Griffe,* 30 May 1997) drew attention to the fact that Jean-Pierre Poughon, the manager of Leroy Gabon, was a 'convicted criminal' who had been sentenced to 20 years' imprisonment in the Ivory Coast for 'irregular business practice', before he moved to Gabon.

Furthermore, while Leroy's certification was the subject of a major dispute at the FSC, Poughon quickly ordered a dramatic increase in production volume from 5,600 m^3 of timber per month to 13,000 m^3 per month, whereas the maximum monthly volume allowed by the Gabonese authorities was 4,500 m^3 (*La Griffe,* 30 May 1997). To accomplish this new production target, working hours were increased and a Sunday shift was introduced.

In view of the issues outlined above which were clearly articulated in protest letters, the FSC board finally ruled in favour of the complainants on 2 October 1997. The board decided that: (i) Leroy Gabon's certificate and right to use an FSC-backed ecolabel for marketing its wood be revoked immediately; (ii) SGS should be publicly sanctioned for performance not in compliance with FSC principles and criteria; and (iii) the chairperson of the FSC board of directors review its procedure for handling complaints with the assistance of an outside consultant.

5.5 Implementing FSC auditing standards: some implications of the Leroy Gabon case

The Leroy Gabon case reveals a number of areas where institutional arrangements that currently exist for financial audits are remarkably similar to those which have evolved in forest stewardship audits. In particular, many of the problems associated with financial audit procedures (e.g. establishment of auditing standards, qualifications in audit reports, expectations gap, problems of independence etc.), and their organisational impact (e.g. in relation to corporate governance) also arise in the context of forest stewardship audits.

The FSC's formalised auditing procedures embodied in its principles and criteria constitute a social construction of auditability in line with Hines (1989) and Power (1997a). For example, Power (1997a, p. 309) notes: 'not only do audits create and reinforce the conditions for their own functioning, but they seek to do so by creating a new bureaucratic 'surface' or social reality which is highly standardised and which represents the auditee for the purpose of the audit'.

This social constructivism could, to some extent, explain the major dispute regarding interpretation of FSC principles in the Leroy Gabon case from the standpoint of forest auditors (SGS), stakeholders (e.g. Friends of the Earth, Rainforest Alliance, and other environmental campaigners), and the FSC itself. Furthermore, it not only suggests an implicit 'expectations gap' between the social and environmental objectives of stakeholders and those that are achievable via FSC-based audits, but also portrays the kind of ambiguity associated with the British 'true and fair view' audit qualification.

Whereas most UK-style financial audit reports indicate whether or not accounting reports portray a 'true and fair view', FSC-based audits indicate whether or not forests are 'well managed'. Also, just as there is a general presumption that compliance with generally accepted accounting standards would lead to a 'true and fair view', there is a presumption that compliance with FSC principles would mean that a forest *is* 'well managed'.

In order to define the phrase 'well managed', a series of public consultations were initiated by the FSC in 1993 that included formal hearings in Malaysia, Sweden, Peru, the United States, and six other countries (Upton and Bass, 1996). In addition, FSC working parties comprising experts in economic, environmental, and social issues, from both industrialised countries and less developed countries, carried out a large-scale questionnaire survey and subsequently convened on a number of occasions to revise draft 'principles' based on the information received. At least one of these principles was revised over nine times before being overwhelmingly approved by a formal vote in 1994. The broad range of countries and social constituencies represented in the FSC General Assembly – producers, traders, retailers, consumer groups, indigenous peoples, environmentalists, etc. – highlight the social construction of auditability here.

Some critics (e.g. Kiekens, 1997, p. 19) have argued that the FSC's auditing and ecolabelling schemes are neither necessary nor sufficient to achieve sustainable forest management because commercial logging is not the only factor that causes tropical deforestation. He points out that other important factors that play a vital role include expansion of agriculture, expansion of ranching, weakness of the tenure system, uncontrolled fires, development of the mining sector, construction of dams etc. Kiekens goes on to argue that, by presenting FSC ecolabels as tantamount to sustainable forest management, international agencies such as the World Bank, the European Union, and the Lomé Convention have de-emphasised the fundamental issues.

Furthermore, some interest groups (e.g. the Timber Trade Federation, the American Forest and Paper Association, small forest managers etc.) have developed their own forest auditing standards, with different definitions of 'well managed', in order to avoid the perceived undesirable economic consequences of the FSC approach (see, e.g., Urry, 1997). For example, WWF (1994, p. 19) explains:

> One might think that moves to improve the sustainability of forestry and timber trading would have been joined wholeheartedly by the trade and their representatives. However, in general the timber trade is a proud and deeply conservative business, and has not taken kindly to criticism. The frustration felt by environmentalists who have seen the horrors of unsustainable logging has increasingly led to acrimony and, on occasion, diversion from the most important issues.

Although the lack of agreement or consensus over the definition of 'well managed' has led to a proliferation of ecolabelling and certification schemes, the FSC model is currently the only one recommended by WWF, the World Bank, and the European Union. The social constructivist nature of these forest auditing schemes might suggest that they portray a form of ideological 'green washing' and also present some of the problems associated with financial audits identified by Power (1995, pp. 320–1):

> With the possible exception of statistical sampling, auditing does not seem to have a knowledge base.... Thus, the consensus of 'more experienced' auditors in performing an audit task which is well defined in the professional literature merely tells us that they are capable of reproducing officially sanctioned programmes based upon prescribed procedures. If we have doubts about the knowledge system which is constituted by these accepted procedures, then such a consensus is of little value. Indeed, in such circumstances, it may be the minority dissenting judgements which deserve intellectual attention.

5.6 New public management and forest stewardship auditing

FSC principles and criteria encompass the establishment of management plans, forestry policy, land tenure and use rights, protection of the rights of indigenous people and local communities, environmental impact assessment and monitoring among a broad range of other issues set out in Table 5.1. In Gabon (as in most other countries), these matters would normally fall within the jurisdiction of the Ministry of Forest and Water Resources. However, an independent audit of forest management processes based upon FSC principles would suggest a major shift in the environmental management function from state bureaucracy to management control mechanisms within forestry companies.

These developments were not well received by Gabonese forestry authorities, who actively supported the move by environmental campaigners to decertify Leroy Gabon and strip off its FSC-backed ecolabel. Bayami (1997, p. 3) explains:

> We strongly oppose the approach this company had chosen: that of excluding from the process, at the national level, the partners of the land, in particular, the forestry authorities, NGOs, and the local population.... Therefore, at the level of Gabon, neither the forestry administration nor national NGOs were involved during consultations and this, deliberately. This constitutes for us a lack of respect/consideration for the Gabonese authorities and other partners in the sector.

Similar concerns were noted by Knight (1997, p. 2):

> Before FSC's withdrawal of certification for Leroy Gabon, Gabon's Water and Forest Department expressed concern that they were not involved in the process. 'Such things should not be secret to the Department, which is a stakeholder in this long and delicate process of certification.'

The forest stewardship audit processes that were carried out in Leroy Gabon's concession by SGS represent a commitment to push control functions away from government departments and further down into organisational structures, in line with the notion of 'internalisation of governance' enunciated by Power (1997a).

As such, the presumed inefficiency of a hierarchical bureaucracy (e.g. the Gabonese government) is replaced by the presumed efficiency of markets. This arrangement can also be analysed in terms of the Foucauldian notion of 'governmentality' which refers to current tendencies for political power to be 'exercised through a profusion of shifting alliances between diverse authorities in projects [e.g. as illustrated in Figure 5.1] to govern a multitude of facets of economic activity, social life, and individual conduct' (Rose and Miller, 1992). Thus, 'governmentality' can be seen as government that emanates from various authorities and organisations. As Power (1997a, p. 43) notes, the term covers 'forms of intervention and control which are more indirect and distant, seeking to act on and through the interests and motivations of subjects and organisations'. In this context, one could see the alliance between private-sector subjects and organisations (e.g. FSC, environmental NGOs, individual 'green' consumers, ethical investors etc.) and diverse authorities (e.g. Lomé Convention, World Bank, and EU) illustrated in Figure 5.1 as a model of govenmentality, the key features of which were described by Power (1997b, p. 125) thus:

> The general idea is that command philosophies of regulation are giving way to forms of control which utilise the cognitive and economic resources of the regulatee. Regulation is increasingly pushed down into organisations and their internal systems of self-assessment and control.

Hence, by compelling tropical countries to adopt the FSC scheme as a condition for structural adjustment assistance or development aid, international agencies such as the World Bank and the EU have effectively attempted to export the New Public Management philosophy, which evolved in OECD countries (see, e.g., Hood, 1991, 1995), to other national settings.

In FSC audits, the auditee bears the cost of the audit in exchange for an ecolabel that would enhance the marketing of its wood products. Another presumed advantage of this arrangement is that, in most tropical countries, there are inadequate prerequisites for sustainable forest management, such as existence of forestry policy and management plan; effective land tenure systems; effective mechanism for protection of the customary rights of indigenous people; capacity for environmental impact assessment etc. (Kiekens, 1997). By 'privatising' such forest management functions via the FSC initiative, the presumed inefficiencies of state bureaucracy will be replaced by the presumed efficiency of 'green' markets. However, a major unresolved problem with the FSC scheme relates to the notion of 'well managed', a phrase which, like the 'true and fair view' qualification in financial audits, is ambiguous and very poorly defined.

5.7 Conclusion

This chapter has examined the impact of auditing and ecolabelling strategies on governance arrangements in the forestry industry, using evidence from a case study of Leroy Gabon's logging concession. It was made evident that consumer-driven forest management audits sanctioned by the FSC could shift much of the responsibility for sustainable forest management from state bureaucracy to management control mechanisms within forest exploitation companies.

The tensions between claims to professionalism by the FSC and its accredited auditors and sustainability concerns of committed environmental campaigners noted here seem to suggest that, left to their own devices, companies could actively use corporate social disclosures and ecolabels to legitimate their operations or to deflect undesirable stakeholder demands.

In summary, the Leroy Gabon case study has demonstrated that, in some respects, corporate social responsibility activities and disclosures can be seen as part of a strategic posture adopted to actively defend a company's (enlightened) self-interests.

5.8 Summary of key points

Forest Stewardship Council-based audits portray the following features.

- Corporate accountability to stakeholders is assessed in terms of nine principles and criteria which were developed on a consensual basis by a broad range of stakeholders from many countries around the world.
- FSC-backed ecolabels are used, in addition to audit reports, to signal clean audits to stakeholders.
- In the FSC model, auditing and corporate social accounting functions are combined. The forest auditor also prepares a corporate social report.
- FSC-based audits are generally voluntary and market-driven, although they are increasingly recommended to tropical countries by the World Bank as a condition for structural adjustment assistance.
- FSC-based audits could shift much of the responsibility for sustainable forest management from state bureaucracy to management control mechanisms within forest exploitation companies.
- Many of the problems associated with financial audit procedures (e.g. establishment of auditing standards, qualifications in audit reports, expectations gap, auditor independence etc.) also arise in FSC-based audits.
- In FSC-based audits, the phrase 'well managed' is analogous to the 'true and fair view' audit qualification in financial audits. These audit qualifications are ambiguous and very poorly defined.
- Some logging companies that feel threatened by 'green' consumers and buyer cartels see FSC-based audits as part of a strategic posture intended to defend their sectional interests as opposed to the public interest.

References

Bayami, A (1997), 'On the Certification of Leroy Gabon', *AFAN Newsletter,* African Forest Action Network, 6, February–March, p. 3.

Eba'a Atyi, R (1997), 'La Certification des Forêts: Le Cas du Cameroun', *Bois et Forêts des Tropiques,* 253:3, pp. 62–6.

Hall, W (1997) 'Pakistan SGS Ahead but Warns on Year', *Financial Times, 23* September, p. 30.

Hall, W, Bokhari, F and Burns, J (1997) 'Executive Suspended in Bhutto Probe: Swiss Company Investigates Allegations of Corruption in its Pakistan Operations', *Financial Times, 23* September, p. 3.

Hansen, E (1997), 'Forest Certification and its Role in Marketing Strategy', *Forest Products Journal,* 47:3, pp. 16–22.

Hines, R (1989), 'Financial Accounting Knowledge, Conceptual Framework Projects, and the Social Construction of the Accounting Profession', *Accounting, Auditing and Accountability Journal,* 2:2, pp. 72–92.

Hood, C (1991), 'Public Management for all Seasons?', *Public Administration,* 69, pp. 3–19.

Hood, C (1995), 'The New Public Management in the 1980s: Variations on a Theme', *Accounting, Organisations, and Society,* 20:2/3, pp. 93–109.

Kiekens, J P (1997), 'Certification: International Trends and Forestry Trade Implications', Study Presented by Environmental Strategies Europe to the Ministère de l'Environnement des Ressources Naturelles et de l'Agriculture de la Région Wallone, Brussels.

Knight, D (1997), 'Forest Council Takes Action against Logging Company in Gabon', InterPress Service, Internet posting, 21 November.

Power, M (1995), 'Auditing, Expertise, and the Sociology of Technique', *Critical Perspectives on Accounting,* 6, pp. 317–39.

Power, M (1997a), *The Audit Society: Rituals of Verification,* Oxford, Oxford University Press.

Power, M (1997b), 'Expertise and the Construction of Relevance: Accountants and Environmental Audit', *Accounting, Organisations, and Society,* 22:2, pp. 123–46.

Roberts, R (1998), 'A Stakeholder Approach to the Corporate Single Audit', *Critical Perspectives on Accounting,* 9, pp. 227–32.

Rose, N and Miller, P (1992), 'Political Power beyond the State: Problematics of Government', *British Journal of Sociology,* 2, pp. 173–205.

Ullmann, A, 'Data in Search of a Theory: a Critical Examination of the Relationship among Social Performance, Social Disclosure and Economic Performance', *Academy of Management Review,* pp. 540–77.

Upton, C and Bass, S (1996), *The Forest Certification Handbook,* London, Earthscan.

Urry, M (1997), 'World Pulp and Paper: Sustainable Forests – Overcoming Growing Pains', *Financial Times,* 8 December, p. 3.

World Wide Fund For Nature (1994), *Truth or Trickery? Timber Labelling Past and Future,* UK, WWF.

World Wide Fund For Nature (1996), *The 1995 Group: The Full Story,* UK, WWF.

6

Evaluation of Policy and Practice

This chapter draws together key strands of the preceding chapters in order to: (i) show how this study complements the theoretical model for costing environmental sustainability that was proposed by Bebbington and Gray (1997); and (ii) evaluate the OCAM Plan's conceptual framework against the backdrop of ongoing IASC and ACCA projects on accounting in developing countries.

6.1 Accounting for sustainability

The recent emergence of sustainability as a new theoretical challenge within which to reconfigure social and environmental accounting was highlighted by Gray (1995, p. 4):

> At least, now, environmental and social accounting issues are attracting some of the wealth of talent available in accounting academe, and this is bringing an increasing rigour to bear on the way in which problems are expressed and addressed.

However, the ways in which sustainability concerns were incorporated into the design of the OCAM Plan have not yet reached the extant environmental accounting literature. Sustainability was defined in the Brundtland Report in terms of development which meets the needs of the present without compromising the ability of future generations to meet their own needs (UNWCED, 1987). This broad definition was used to reconceptualise the Hicksian notion of income and capital maintenance in an environmental accounting context. Thus, a sustainable business was defined as one which leaves the environment no worse off at the end of each accounting period than it was at the beginning of that accounting period.

There are two main components of sustainability which are of interest here, namely eco-efficiency (i.e. issues relating to the physical environment and mankind's use of it) and eco-justice (i.e. intra/inter-generational equity and related social issues). Chapters 3 and 4 analysed the role played by the OCAM Plan in resolving some of these problems.

6.2 Costing environmental sustainability

In many respects, the OCAM model complements the key issues that Bebbington and Gray (1997) tackled in their study of the Landcare experimental project in New

Zealand, which used the idea of sustainable cost calculation to envisage what a sustainable organisation could look like from an eco-efficiency standpoint. Essentially, they attempted to accomplish a shift from the unsustainable position portrayed by conventional accounting to what they arbitrarily described as the most sustainable option available by incorporating the costs of purchasing environmentally sound inputs and of remedying environmental damage (see Figure 6.1).

Figure 6.1 Stages in costing environmental sustainability

(a) Present position	(b) Most sustainable operation currently available	(c) Zero environmental impact	(d) Past damage remedied
Unsustainable operations	Most sustainable operations		Fully sustainable operations

(*Source:* Bebbington and Tan (1996, p. 76))

In order to effect the shift from an unsustainable position to a more sustainable option – i.e. from point (a) to point (b) in Figure 6.1 – the OCAM Plan adopts a pragmatic approach based upon the internalisation of externalities via taxation, as analysed in Chapter 4.

Furthermore, it was explained in Chapter 4 that the OCAM model addresses social justice (or eco-justice) matters by placing emphasis on the notion of value added.[1] For instance, substantial tax concessions are granted to companies that generate high levels of value added. Another manifestation of this emphasis on value added relates to the forest tax statutes which clearly spell out the modalities for allocating tax revenues to stakeholders such as village communities, councils and central government, thereby seeking to alleviate some eco-justice problems.

It can also be argued that the Forest Stewardship Council's auditing scheme discussed in Chapter 5 offers another insight into the solution to the problem illustrated in Figure 6.1, since the costs incurred in effecting the shift from (a) towards (b) and (c) are internalised within the logging company. Indeed, the FSC's principles and criteria set out in Table 5.1 cover key eco-justice matters such as protection of the customary rights of indigenous peoples, land tenure, sustainable forest management plans, and environmental impact assessment.

However, just as it is impossible to achieve (c) and (d) in Figure 6.1 using Bebbington and Gray's approach, some critics have argued that the FSC model is an unattainable ideal. For example, Reeve (1993) points out:

---

1 See Elad and Gray (1991) or Elad (1995) for a more detailed discussion of the OCAM notion of value added.

> The statement [FSC Principle 6] that forest management must 'minimise' not prevent adverse environmental impacts pays lip service to conservation needs. In reality, a full assessment of the impact of cutting down forests, even selectively, cannot be made for at least 70 years after the event, by which time it will be too late.... Neither is acknowledgement made of the unique nature and importance of tropical forests with regard to biodiversity maintenance or our profound lack of knowledge.

6.3 Relevance of the OCAM model

The main objective of this study was to evaluate the extent to which the government's strategy whereby accounting is intertwined with economic development policy has stimulated sustainability in the forestry sector. It was found that there are three main reasons why this arrangement portrays the hallmarks of an accounting model that was designed to enhance sustainability.

First, it was shown in the preceding section that, while perfect sustainability is obviously an unachievable ideal, the OCAM approach, coupled with the Forest Stewardship Council auditing scheme, has effected a shift from the unsustainable position portrayed by conventional accounting to point (b) on the sustainability spectrum in Figure 6.1.

Second, the framework of the OCAM Plan compels companies to disclose information that is used to support environmental management, macroeconomic planning, and fiscal policy decision-making. In particular, it incorporates extensive natural resource accounting information relating to minerals, chemicals, metals, livestock, wildlife, forests etc. in volume and in monetary terms. This information can be used to monitor the rate of depletion of natural resources that can be attributed to the operations of large multinational companies.

Third, although the tax incentives granted to companies on the basis of accounting disclosures generated by the OCAM Plan resulted in the expropriation of national resources by foreign multinationals over the period 1960–94, the authorities have now revised and streamlined the tax regime to ensure that it supports sustainable development. For example, the 1997 Finance Law instituted a dramatic increase in all forest taxes and a requirement that tax incentives be linked to the level of local corporate value added. The strong emphasis on the notion of value added could also be seen in terms of the way in which tax revenue is allocated to social constituencies.

In summary, although very little is known about it in the Anglo-Saxon world, the OCAM Plan was developed from a conceptual framework which was specifically structured to address the objectives of accounting and financial reporting in the developing countries concerned. Unlike the narrow 'decision usefulness' orientation of Anglo-Saxon conceptual frameworks – such as those developed by the ASB, IASC or FASB – the OCAM conceptual framework adopted a broader perspective which emphasised the needs of a wide range of stakeholders. The implementation of this model in Cameroon shows how OCAM accounting is intertwined with environmental management, macroeconomic planning, and fiscal policy.

6.4 Implications for the literature on accounting in developing countries

Nobes (1998) attempted to identify some desirable features of an accounting system that is relevant to developing countries. It is interesting to note that the OCAM Plan portrays most of these desirable features. For example, Nobes (1998, pp. 28–9) argues that an accounting model that supports reporting to tax authorities is likely to be more appropriate to many developing countries than the Anglo-Saxon model. He also points out that the unique requirements of some industries which are more important in developing countries than in the industrialised countries (e.g. extractive industries, agriculture, forestry etc.) may warrant industry-specific accounting standards which are substantially different from those that normally feature in the IASC's standardisation agenda.

6.5 Summary of key points

Summing up, it is noteworthy that the conceptual framework of the OCAM Plan takes care of the following key research questions on accounting in developing countries that were raised in the ACCA report by Nobes (1998, pp. 37–40):

- How could one define the efficiency of a tax reporting system?
- Are the economies in developing countries biased towards certain industries which are less important in developed countries?
- To what extent is the IASC framework inappropriate to users (other than investors in public companies), and what does this imply about appropriate accounting standards?
- Is tax reporting an important (or perhaps most important) use of accounting in developing countries?
- Should the IASC (or some other body) create a system of accounting procedures for use in countries with few accountants and few public companies?
- Are important industries left without guidance?
- Is the present author (i.e. Nobes) right to conclude that the IASC does not need to pay much attention to issues (d) to (g) (as enumerated at the beginning of Chapter 2 here), except for issuing guidance on the application of existing standards?

References

Bebbington, J and Gray, R H (1997), 'An Account of Sustainability: Failure, Success and a Reconceptualisation', Fifth Interdisciplinary Perspectives on Accounting Conference, Vol. 1, University of Manchester, Manchester, July.

Bebbington, J and Tan, J (1996), 'Accounting for Sustainability', *Chartered Accountants Journal,* July, pp. 75–6.

Elad, C M (1995), 'The Value Added Accounting Principles of the OCAM Plan: A Theoretical Appraisal', *Research in Accounting in Emerging Economies,* Vol. 3, pp. 53–82.

Elad, C M and Gray, S J (1991), 'Value Added Accounting in Equatorial Africa', Paper presented at the 1991 Congress of the European Accounting Association, University of Limburg, Maastricht, The Netherlands.

Gray, R H (1995), 'Social and Environmental Accounting Research', Briefings from the GEC Programme, *Global Environmental Change Programme Briefings,* No. 5, September.

Nobes, C (1998), *Accounting in Developing Economies: Questions about Users, Uses and Appropriate Reporting Practices,* London, ACCA.

Reeve, R (1993), 'The Forest Stewardship Council Aims, Principles and Criteria: A Critical Examination Predicting its Failure', Paper presented at the Founding Assembly meeting of the FSC, Toronto.

United Nations World Commission on Environment and Development (1987), *Our Common Future* (The Brundtland Report), UNWCED, Oxford, Oxford University Press.

Appendix 1

The OCAM Industrial Classification for Goods and Services

01 Agricultural, stock breeding and hunting products
02 Silvicultural and forestry products
03 Fishing products
04 Meat and preserved meat
05 Milk products
06 Preserved fruits, vegetables and fish
07 Fats
08 Products of the grain industry
09 Sugar
10 Bakery and pastry products
11 Other food products and prepared animal foods
12 Alcoholic drinks
13 Soft drinks
14 Manufactured tobacco
15 Solid mineral fuels
16 Crude petroleum products and natural gas
17 Refined petroleum products
18 Cooking products
19 Electricity
20 Gas, steam
21 Water
22 Iron ore
23 Non-ferrous ores
24 Iron metallurgy products and steel basic industries
25 Non-ferrous metals and the first workings of non-ferrous metals
26 Fabricated metal products, except machinery and equipment
27 Machinery except electrical
28 Electrical machinery and appliances
29 Motor vehicles and cycles
30 Railway equipment
31 Aircraft
32 Ships
33 Professional and scientific equipment not elsewhere classified
34 Other products of mining not elsewhere classified
35 Constructional and ceramic materials
36 Glass and glass products
37 Basic chemical products
38 Other chemical products
39 Rubber products and articles
40 Plastic products and articles
41 Textiles
42 Wearing apparel
43 Leather and products of leather
44 Wood and worked wood (except furniture)
45 Furniture
46 Pulp, paper and processed paper
47 Printing, newspapers and publishing industries products
48 Other manufacturing industries products
49 Constructions
50 Land transport services
51 Water transport services
52 Air transport services
53 Ancillary transport services
54 Telecommunications services
(55–56)........
57 Ancillary agricultural services
58 Restaurants and cafés and other eating and drinking places
59 Hotels and other lodging places
60 Real and landed estate services
61 Business services
62 Repair services not elsewhere classified
63 Laundry cleaning and dyeing services
64 Domestic services
65 Personal services not elsewhere classified

Appendix 2

Statistics and Tax Return Form

STANDARD

MODEL

STATISTICS AND TAX RETURN

Period from ____________ to ____________

Firm's or proprietor's name ____________

Initial letters. abbreviated name or mark ____________

P.O. Box ____________ Town ____________

Phone ____________

SCIFE registration number	

LEGAL AND FISCAL STATUS (see headings over leaf)

Legal status ____________

Nature of the firm ____________

Fiscal status ____________

Approvals obtained ____________

Individual Business only — Nature of profits ____________

Nationality of firm's manag. ____________

FIRM'S ACTIVITIES

		Percentage of overall turnover
Main Activity at the beginning and closing of the period	____________	%
	____________	
Other Activities at the beginning and closing of the period	____________	%
	____________	%
	____________	%
	____________	%
New activities engaged in during the period	____________	%
	____________	%
Activities given up during the period	____________	%
If the firm has ceased operations, state why	____________	%

Statistics and tax return drawn up by ____________

Appendix 3

Provisions and Deductible Provisions Form

STANDARD MODEL

Period ______________________ TABLE 6

Business Name ______________________

ADM. ONLY | 1 | 1 | | | | | | | | | | 0 | 0 | | | | | | | | | | |

TABLE OF PROVISIONS								
No GAP	HEADINGS	Line (12 13)	Opening balances of provisions accounts 1 (14–24)	Provisions made during the period (or other increases)		Provisions written back (or other decreases)		Closing balances of provisions a/c 6 (69–79)
				Deductible 2 (25–35)	Non deduct. 3 (36–46)	Deductible 4 (47–57)	Non deduct. 5 (58–68)	
013	Regulated provisions	01						
013	Gains on dispos. to be reinvest	02						
019	P. for long term liab. & contin.	03						
029	P. for loss in val. of fixed and long term assets	04						
039	P. for loss in val. of stocks	05						
049	P. for losses in respect of third party accounts	06						
059	P. for losses in respect of financial accounts	07						
	TOTAL : lines 1 to 7	08						

PARTICULARS OF DEDUCTIBLE PROVISIONS

NATURE	REASONS	AMOUNTS

Appendix 4

Purchases of Raw Materials and Stores Form

STANDARD MODEL

Period ______________________ TABLE 12

Business Name ______________________

ADM. ONLY | 1 | 9 | (boxes 1 2 4 9 11) | 0 | 0 | (boxes 12 13 14)

TABLE OF PURCHASES OF RAW MATERIALS AND STORES

HEADINGS	Line (12 13)	Classification Number (14 1 18)	Made in Cameroon (net price) (20 2 27)	Made directly abroad (CIF): UDEAC (28 3 35)	Made directly abroad (CIF): other countries (36 4 43)	TOTAL (44 5 51)
	01					
	02					
	03					
	04					
	05					
	06					
	07					
	08					
	09					
	10					
	11					
	12					
	13					
	14					
	15					
	16					
	17					
	18					
	19					
	20					
	21					
	22					
	23					
	24					
	25					
Sundry Unclassification	26	9 4 0 0 Q				
Sundry Unclassified	27	9 6 0 0 H				
TOTALS lines 1-27 7	28	9 7 0 0 R				

TABLE OF EXPENSES RELATING TO THE PURCHASES

	12 13	20 27	28	43	44 51
Customs duties	29				
Transit expenses	30				
Transp. expenses	31				
Trans. Insur. premium	32				
Commissions on purchases	33				
Other expenses	34				
TOTALS lines 29-34	35				

Total purchases c/d (line 28 col. 5)		
Total expenses c/d (line 35 col. 5)		
PURCHASE COST TOTAL		
Raw mat. & stores opening stock		
Packing mat. opening stock		
Opening stock in transit		
OPENING STOCK TOTAL	+	
Raw mat. & stores closing stock		
Packing mat. closing stock		
Closing stock in transit		
CLOSING STOCK TOTAL	−	
RAW MATERIALS AND STORES CONSUMED	=	

Appendix 5

Output of Goods or Services Form

STANDARD MODEL

Period______________________________ TABLE 13A

Business Name______________________________

ADM. ONLY | 2 | 0 | … | 0 | 0 | …

TABLE OF OUTPUT OF GOODS OR SERVICES IN VALUE – 1st PART					
			OUTPUT SOLD (ACCOUNTS 71/071)		
				ABROAD	
HEADINGS	Line	Classification Number 1	OUTPUT SOLD TOTAL 2 = 3 + 4 + 7	UDEAC 3	OTHER COUNTRIES 4
	01				
	02				
	03				
	04				
	05				
	06				
	07				
	08				
	09				
	10				
	11				
	12				
	13				
	14				
	15				
	16				
	17				
	18				
Sundry unclassified	19	9 6 0 0 H			
TOTALS lines 1 to 19	20	9 7 0 0 R			

TABLE OF OUTPUT OF GOODS IN QUANTITY					
HEADINGS	Line	Classification Number	TOTAL SOLD	UDEAC	OTHER COUNTRIES
	21				
	22				
	23				
	24				
	25				
	26				
	27				
	28				
	29				
	30				

Appendix 6

Personnel Expenses Form

STANDARD MODEL

Period ______________ TABLE 19

Business Name ______________

ADM. ONLY 2 7 / 0 0

TABLE OF PERSONNEL EXPENSES (ACCOUNTS 65/665)

HEADINGS	Line		INCURRED IN CAMEROON: Cameroonians 1	INCURRED IN CAMEROON: Other Africans 2	INCURRED IN CAMEROON: Others 3	INCURRED IN CAMEROON: TOTAL 4=1+2+3	INCURRED ABROAD 5	TOTAL 6=4+5
Permanent Staff: Manual labour	01							
Permanent Staff: Clerks & sales agents	02							
Permanent Staff: Executive, supervisors & foremen	03							
TEMPORARY Staff	04							
TOTALS lines 1 to 4	05							
Transport and lodging allowances	06							
Other social allowances	07							
WAGES & SOCIAL ALLOWANCES : TOTALS line 5 - 7	08							
CNPS Contributions	09							
Other social contributions	10							
FRINGE BENEFITS IN KIND: Food	11							
FRINGE BENEFITS IN KIND: Water, gas, electricity	12							
FRINGE BENEFITS IN KIND: Uniforms, medicines	13							
FRINGE BENEFITS IN KIND: Leave transports	14							
FRINGE BENEFITS IN KIND: Lodging	15							
FRINGE BENEFITS IN KIND: Medical and sundry services	16							
FRINGE BENEFITS IN KIND: Other benefits	17							
FRINGE BENEFITS IN KIND: TOTALS lines 11 to 17	18							
TOTALS lines 8, 9, 10 & 18	19							

SUM RECEIVED BY STAFF (recorded in various accounts)

	Line				
TOTALS lines 8 carried down	20				
Notional or proportional business travelling allowance	21				
National entertainment allowances	22				
Other sums received shown elsewhere in the return	23				
SUMS RECEIVED BY STAFF : TOTALS lines 20 - 23	24				

Appendix 7

Rates and Taxes Form

STANDARD MODEL

Period ______________ TABLE 20

Business Name ______________

ADM. ONLY | 1 2 | 8 | | 0 | 0 |

RATES AND TAXES (ACCOUNTS 66/066)						
HEADINGS	Line 12 13		Payable in the State 20 1 27	Payable to intern. organ. 28 2 35	Payable abroad 36 3 43	TOTAL 44 4 51
Business licences	01					
Apprenticeship tax	02					
Council tax	03					
Cattle tax	04					
Internal turnover tax	05					
Registration taxes	06					
Fiscal stamps	07					
Stamp duty	08					
Forest tax	09					
Tax on firm's capital	10					
Vehicle licence owner. cert.	11					
Tax on insurance contract	12					
Single tax	13					
National manufactur. tax	14					
Stabilisation funds withdraw.	15					
Exp. customs duties (goods)	16					
Exp. customs duties (sces)	17					
Deductible fiscal penalties and fines	18					
Non-deductible fiscal penalties and fines	19					
Unclassified sundry rates and taxes	20					
TOTALS lines 1 to 20	21					

FIRMS RECORDING TURNOVER. TAX EXCLUDED	12 13	20	27
Amount of internal turnover tax not included in a/c 66/066	22		

INTEREST PAID (ACCOUNT 67/067)					
HEADINGS	Line 12 13		to organs. Cameroon 1 27	to organs. abroad 28 2 35	TOTAL 36 3 43
Bond and debenture interest	23				
Redemption premiums	24				
Interest on other borrowings repayable after more than 1 yr.	25				
Interest on borrowings repayable within one year	26				
Interest on partners current a/c	27				
Bank interest	28				
Discounts granted	29				
Sundry	30				
TOTALS lines 23 to 30	31				

Appendix 8

Revenue and Profits Form

STANDARD MODEL

Period ______________ TABLE 21

Business Name ______________

ADM. ONLY 2 9 (1 2 4 9 11) — 0 0 (12 13 14)

SUNDRY REVENUE AND PROFITS (ACCOUNTS 74/074)					
NATURE / ORIGIN	Line (12 13)		Earned in Cameroon (20) 1 (27)	Earned abroad (28) 2 (35)	TOTAL (36) 3 (43)
Rebates, refunds & dis. obtained	01				
Allowances obtained from customer	02				
Sales premiums & forfeited deposit	03				
Royalties on patents & licences	04				
Subscriptions & donations received	05				
Apportion of invest. grant & subsidies	06				
Recoveries in resp. of debts previously written off	07				
Exchange defferences	08				
Fire & sundry risks insur. compens.	09				
Life insurance compensations	10				
Profits on return of consigned packaging	11				
Sundry 1 ______	12				
Sundry 2 ______	13				
Sundry 3 ______	14				
TOTALS lines 1 to 14	15				

OPERATING, BALANCING AND INVESTMENT SUBSIDIES & GRANTS RECEIVED (A/C 76/076 & 014)					
ORIGIN / NATURE	Line (12 13)		Investment subsidies (20) 1 (27)	Operating and balancing subsidies (28) 2 (35)	Payments from stabilisation fund (36) 3 (43)
The State	16				
Local bodies	17				
National public organisation	18				
National private firm or organ.	19				
Foreign private firm or organ.	20				
International organisation	21				
Other ______	22				
TOTALS lines 16 to 22	23				

INTEREST AND DIVIDENDS EARNED (ACCOUNTS 77/077)					
NATURE / ORIGIN	Line (12 13)		Earned in Cameroon (20) 1 (27)	Earned abroad (28) 2 (35)	TOTAL (36) 3 (43)
Revenue from bonds	24				
Dividends	25				
Interest on loans granted for more than 1 year	26				
Interest on loans granted for less than 1 year	27				
Interest on current accounts	28				
Discount obtained	29				
Directors' fees earned by the firm	30				
Shares of profit earned by the firm	31				
Other interest	32				
TOTALS 24 to 32	33				

Appendix 9

Firm's Structure Form

STANDARD MODEL Period ______________ TABLE 25

Business Name ______________

ADM. ONLY 3 3 (1 2 4 8 9 11) 0 0 (12 13 14)

FIRM'S STRUCTURE : Breakdown per establishment

HEADINGS		Line	Establishment No........	Establishment No........	Establishment No........	Establishment No.........	Establishment No........	Establishment No............
	Name of establishment	01						
		02						
	Town	03						
	P.O. Box	04						
	SCIFE Number	05						
	Creation date of establishment	06						
	Main activity	07						
		08						
No of PERMENENT STAFF	CAMEROONIAN STAFF							
	Manual labour	09						
	Clerks	10						
	Executives & foremen	11						
	TOTALS lines 9 to 11	12						
	OTHER STAFF							
	Manuel labour	13						
	Clerks	14						
	Executives and foremen	15						
	TOTALS lines 13 to 15	16						
	CASUAL staff: No. days worked	17						
	Investments made per establishment	18						
	Turn over	19						
Industrial firms only	Main product manufactured	20						
		21						
	Quantities manufactured	22						

Appendix 10

Tax Base (FOB Price) by Species and Three Geographical Segments - 1997/98

High-value species

OCAM Code	Local name	Scientific name	Zone 1 CFA Francs/M³	Zone 2 CFA Francs/M³	Zone 3 CFA Francs/M³
44 03 34 61	Mahogany (Bassam)	Khaya ivorensis	136,500	130,000	123,500
44 03 99 02	Afromosia/Assamela/Obang	Pericopsis elata	223,672	213,021	202,370
44 03 99 72	Aningré	Aningeria robusta	241,500	230,000	218,500
44 03 35 20	Bété/Mansonia	Mansonia Altissima	131,250	125,000	118,750
44 03 99 09	Bossé	Gaurea cedrata	115,500	110,000	104,500
44 03 99 10	Bubinga	Guibourtia tessmanii	198,404	188,956	179,508
44 03 35 40	Dibetou/Bobolo	Lovoa trichilioides	110,250	105,000	99,750
44 03 99 13	Doussié	Afzelia bipindensis	273,000	260,000	247,000
44 03 99 45	Doussié Blanc	Afzelia pachyloba	157,500	150,000	142,500
44 03 99 14	Ebony	Diospyros spp	232,050	221,000	209,950
44 03 34 80	lroko	Chlorophora excelsa	136,500	130,000	123,500
44 03 99 77	Longhi/Abam	Gambeya africana	241,500	230,000	218,500
44 03 34 70	Makoré/Douka	Tieghemeila africana	89,250	85,000	80,750
44 03 99 25	Moabi	Baillonella toxisperma	126,000	120,000	114,000
44 03 99 26	Movingui	Distemonanthus benthamianus	110,250	105,000	99,750
44 03 99 51	Ovengnkol	Guibourtia ehié	101,850	97,000	92,150
44 03 99 33	Padouk	Pterocarpus soyauxii	110,250	105,000	99,750
44 03 99 34	Pau Rosa	Swartzia fistuloides	153,300	146,000	138,700
44 03 34 40	Sapelli	Entandrophragma cylindricum	157,500	150,000	142,500
44 03 34 50	Sipo	Entandrophragma utile	183,750	175,000	166,250
44 03 99 70	Wenge	Millettia laurentii	147,000	140,000	133,000
44 03 99 37	Zingana/Amuk	Microberlinia bisulcata	115,500	110,000	104,500

Low-value species

OCAM Code	Local name	Scientific name	Zone 1 CFA Francs/M³	Zone 2 CFA Francs/M³	Zone 3 CFA Francs/M³
44 03 34 30	Ayous/Obéché	Triplochyton scleroxylon	105,000	100,000	95,000
44 03 35 61	Azobé/Bongossi	Lophira alata	81,900	78,000	74,100
44 03 99 08	Bilinga	Nauclea diderrichii	84,000	80,000	76,000
44 03 99 16	Framiré	Terminalia ivorensis	89,250	85,000	80,750
44 03 99 20	Kossipo	Entandrophragma candollei	94,500	90,000	85,500
44 03 99 21	Kotibe	Nesogordonia papaverifera	89,250	85,000	80,750
44 03 99 46	Koto	Pterygota macrocarpa	89,250	85,000	80,750
44 03 34 11	Okoumé	Aucoumea klaineana	57,750	55,000	52,250
44 03 33 00	Teak	Tectona grandis	136,500	130,000	123,500
44 03 35 10	Tiama	Entandrophragma angolense	94,500	90,000	85,500

Promotional species

OCAM Code	Local name	Scientific name	Zone 1 CFA Francs/M³	Zone 2 CFA Francs/M³	Zone 3 CFA Francs/M³
44 03 99 03	Aiélé/Abel	Canarium schweinfurthi	78,750	75,000	71,250
44 03 99 04	Ako/Aloa	Antiaris africana	68,250	65,000	61,750
44 03 99 67	Amvout/Ekong	Trichoscypha acuminata	52,500	50,000	47,500
44 03 99 05	Andoung	Monopetalanthus spp	63,000	60,000	57,000
44 03 99 50	Angueuk	Ongokea gore	52,500	50,000	47,500
44 03 99 59	Asila/Kioro/Omang	Maranthes chrysophylia	52,500	50,000	47,500
44 03 99 06	Avodire	Turreaenthus africanus	52,500	50,000	47,500
44 03 99 68	Bodioa	Anopysis klaineana	52,500	50,000	47,500
44 03 99 65	Cordia/Ebe	Cordia platythyrsa	105,000	100,000	95,000
44 03 99 11	Dabema/Atui	Piptadeniastrum africanum	63,000	60,000	57,000
44 03 99 88	Dambala	Discoglypremna caloneura	52,500	50,000	47,500
44 03 99 58	Diana/Celtis/Odou	Celtis tessmannii	52,500	50,000	47,500
44 03 99 53	Ebiara Abem	Berlinia grandiflora	89,250	85,000	80,750
44 03 99 49	Ekaba	Tertraberlinia bifoliata	89,250	85,000	80,750
44 03 99 89	Ékouné	Coelocaryon preussi	52,500	50,000	47,500
44 03 99 61	Emien/Ekouk	Alstonia bonnei	78,750	75,000	71,250
44 03 99 79	Esak	Albizia glaberrima	52,500	50,000	47,500

Promotional species

OCAM Code	Local name	Scientific name	Zone 1 CFA Francs/M³	Zone 2 CFA Francs/M³	Zone 3 CFA Francs/M³
44 03 99 82	Etimoé	Copafera mildbraedil	52,500	50,000	47,500
44 03 99 86	Evène/Ekop évène	Brachystegia mildbraedii	84,000	80,000	76,000
44 03 99 74	Eveuss/Ngon	Klainedoxa gabonensis	52,500	50,000	47,500
44 03 99 87	Evoula/Vitex	Vitex grandifolia	52,500	50,000	47,500
44 03 99 71	Eyek	Pachyelasma tessmannii	52,500	50,000	47,500
44 03 99 15	Eyong	Eribroma oblogum	79,783	75,984	72,185
44 03 99 43	Faro	Daniell ogea	68,250	65,000	61,750
44 03 99 17	Fromager/Ceiba	Ceiba pentandra	68,250	65,000	61,750
44 03 99 54	Gombé/Ekop gombé	Didelotia letouzeyi	84,000	80,000	76,000
44 03 99 57	Latandza/Evouvous	Albizia ferruginea	84,000	80,000	76,000
44 03 35 30	llomba	Pynanthus angolensis	52,500	50,000	47,500
44 03 99 83	Kanda	Beilschmiedia anacardioides	68,250	65,000	61,750
44 03 99 63	Kapokier/Bombax/Esodum	Bombax buonopozense	64,050	61,000	57,950
44 03 99 84	Kondroti/Ovonga	Rodognaphalon brevicuspe	64,050	61,000	57,950
44 03 99 73	Kumbi/Ekoa	Lannea welwitschii	52,500	50,000	47,500
44 03 99 69	Landa	Erythroxylum mannii	52,500	50,000	47,500
44 03 99 66	Lati/Edjil	Amphimas ferrugineus	52,500	50,000	47,500
44 03 35 50	Limba/Frake	Terminalia superba	68,250	65,000	61,750
44 03 99 56	Limbali	Gilbertiodendron dewevrei	78,750	75,000	71,250
44 03 99 52	Lotofa/Nkanang	Sterculia rhinopetala	72,422	68,973	65,524
44 03 99 47	Mambode/Amouk	Detarium macrocarpum	89,250	85,000	80,750
44 03 99 90	Moambé	Enantia chlorantha	52,500	50,000	47,500
44 03 99 85	Mukulungu	Autranella congolensis	68,250	65,000	61,750
44 03 99 91	Mutondo	Funtumia elastica	52,500	50,000	47,500
44 03 99 42	Naga/Ekop naga	Brachystegia cynometroides	84,000	80,000	76,000
44 03 99 29	Niové	Staudtia kamerunensis	84,000	80,000	76,000
44 03 99 55	Oboto/Abodzok	Mammea africana	78,750	75,000	71,250
44 03 99 48	Okan/Adoum	Cylicodiscus gabonensis	52,500	50,000	47,500
44 03 99 30	Olon/Bongo	Fagara heitzil	71,400	68,000	64,600
44 03 99 44	Onzabili/Angongui	Antrocaryon Klaineanum	63,000	60,000	57,000
44 03 99 62	Osanga/Sikon	Pteleopsis hylodendron	52,500	50,000	47,500
44 03 99 64	Ouochi/Albizia/Angoyeme	Albizia zygia	52,500	50,000	47,500
44 03 99 35	Tchitola	Oxystigma oxyphyllum	57,750	55,000	52,250
44 03 99 76	Tsanya/Akela	Pausinystalia macroceras	52,500	50,000	47,500

Appendix 11

Minimum diameter for sustainable harvesting of timber

OCAM code	Local name	Scientific name	Minimum exploitable diameter (metres)
44 03 34 61	Mahogany	Khaya ivorencia	0.8
44 03 99 36	Agba Tota	Gosweilerodendron balsamiferum	1.0
44 03 99 03	Aiélé	Canarium schweimi farthii	0.8
44 03 99 64	Albizia	Albizia spp	0.5
44 03 99 50	Angueuk	Ongokea gore	0.5
44 03 99 04	Antiaris	Antiaris africana	0.6
44 03 99 06	Avodiré	Turreanthus africana	0.6
44 03 34 30	Ayous	Triplochiton scleroxylon	0.8
44 03 35 61	Azobé bongosis	Lophira alata	0.6
44 03 99 01	Bahia	Mitragyna ciliata	0.6
44 03 35 20	Bete	Mansonia altissima	0.6
44 03 99 08	Bilinga Idigbo	Nauclea dederrichi	0.8
44 03 99 09	Bosse Guarea	Gaurea cedrata	0.8
44 03 99 10	Bubinga	Guibourtia tessmani	0.8
44 03 99 11	Dabema	Piptadeniastrum africana	0.8
44 03 99 43	Daniellia	Daniella spp	0.6
44 03 35 40	Dibetou	Lovoa trichilioides	0.8
44 03 34 70	Douka	Teighemolla africana	0.5
44 03 99 13	Doussié	Afzelia bipindensis	0.8
44 03 99 53	Ebiara	Berlinia spp	0.5
44 03 99 61	Emien	Alstonia spp	0.5
44 03 99 74	Eveus	Klainedoxa gabonensis	0.5
44 03 99 15	Eyong	Eribroma oblonga	0.5
44 03 99 17	Fromager	Ceiba pentandra	0.5
44 03 35 30	llomba caraboard	Pynanthus angolensis	0.6
44 03 34 80	lroko	Chlorofora excelsa	1.0
44 03 99 20	Kossipo	Entandrophragma candollei	0.8
44 03 99 21	Kotibé	Nesogordenia spp	0.5
44 03 99 02	Krokodea	Pericopis elata	0.5
44 03 99 69	Landa	Erythroxylum manii	0.5
44 03 35 50	Limba	Terminalia superba	0.6
44 03 99 56	Limbali	Gilbertodendron dewevrei	0.6
44 03 99 25	Moabi	Baillonella toxisperma	1.0
44 03 99 26	Movingui	Distemonanthus benthamianus	0.6
44 03 99 85	Mukulungu	Autranella congolensis	0.6
44 03 99 65	Mukumaari	Cordia spp	0.6
44 03 99 42	Naga	Brachystegia spp	0.6
44 03 99 29	Niove	Staudia spp	0.5
44 03 99 11	Obeche	Piptadeniastrum	0.8
44 03 99 55	Oboto	Mammea africana	0.5
44 03 99 48	Okan	Cyclicodiscus gabonensis	0.6
44 03 99 30	Olong	Fagara heitzii	0.6
44 03 99 44	Onzabilli	Antrocaryon spp	0.5
44 03 99 32	Ozigo	Dacryodes buettneri	0.5
44 03 99 33	Padouk	Pterocarpus soyauxii	0.6
44 03 99 80	Pau Rosa	Ricinodendron spp	0.5
44 03 99 49	Ribi	Tetraberlinia bifoliolata	0.6
44 03 34 40	Sapelli	Entandophragma cylindricum	1.0
44 03 99 62	Sikon	Pteleopsis hylodendron	0.5
44 03 34 50	Sipo	Entandrophragma utile	0.8
44 03 99 41	Tali	Erythrophleum spp	0.5
44 03 99 35	Tchitchola	Oxystigma oxyplylium	0.6
44 03 35 10	Tiama	Etandrophagma angolensis	0.8
44 03 99 87	Vitex	Vitex spp	0.5
44 03 99 52	Wawabina	Sterculia rhinopetala	0.6

Appendix 12

List of FSC-certified Forests by Country (name of forest auditor given in italics)

Belgium

Heverleebos SA-FM-1050/COC-1051 Soil Association Government Plantation/Semi-natural 635 ha. Meerdaalwoud SA-FM-1052/COC-1053 Soil Association Government Plantation/Semi-natural 1 255 ha. Total for Belgium 1 890 ha.

Belize

Programme for Belize SW-FM/COC-031 Rainforest Alliance Non-Industrial Natural 95 800 ha. Total for Belize 95 800 ha.

Bolivia

Amazonic Sustainable Enterprises, Inc. SW-FM/COC-058 Rainforest Alliance Private Mixed-natural/plantation 30 000 ha. Aserradero Tarumá Ltda. SW-FM/COC-045 Rainforest Alliance Industrial Natural 83 467 ha. Central Intercomunal Campesina del Oriente de Lomerio (CICOL)/ APCOB SW-FM-010 Rainforest Alliance Communal Natural 52 000 ha. Compañia Industrial Maderera Ltda. (CIMAL) SW-FM/COC-036 Rainforest Alliance Industrial Natural 155 466 ha. Empresa Agroindustrial La Chonta Ltda-Concesión La Chonta SW-FM/COC-093 Rainforest Alliance Government Natural 100 000 ha. Empresa Agroindustrial La Chonta Ltda: Concesión Lago Rey SW-FM/COC-050 Rainforest Alliance Industrial Natural 120 000 ha. Empresa Aserradero San Martín S.R.L. Concesion Cinma-San Martin SW-FM/COC-086 Rainforest Alliance Private Natural 119 200 ha. Total for Bolivia 660 133 ha.

Brazil

A. W. Faber-Castell S.A SCS-PM-00005 SCS Private Plantation 8 987 ha. Duratex SA – Botucatu, Lencois Paulistas, & Agudos Districts SCS-PM-00002/COC-00043 SCS Industrial Plantation 47 904 ha. Eucatex SA – Salto & Botucatu and Buri SCS-PM-00001 SCS Industrial Plantation 48 962 ha. Floresteca Agroflorestal Ltda. SGS-FM-0079 SGS Forestry Industrial Plantation 8 519 ha. Flosul Industria e Comercio de Madeiras Ltda. SW-FM/COC-087 Rainforest Alliance Private Plantation 6764 ha. Klabin Fabricadora de Papel e Celulose SA SW-FM/COC-038 Rainforest Alliance Private Plantation 218 545 ha. Mannesmann Florestal Ltda. SGS-FM-0212 SGS Forestry Industrial Plantation 235 886 ha. Mil Madeireira Itacoatiara Ltda. SW-FM-019 Rainforest Alliance Industrial Natural 80 571 ha. Plantar SA SCS-PM-00004/COC-00088 SCS Private Plantation 9 420 ha. Precious Woods Amazon SW-FM/COC-019 Rainforest Alliance Private Natural 80 000 ha. Total for Brazil 1 415 224 ha.

Canada

Haliburton Forest and Wildlife Reserve SW-FM/COC-033 Rainforest Alliance Industrial Natural 19 184 ha. JD Irving Black Brook District SCS-FM-00016 SCS Private Natural 190 890 ha. Tembec, Inc., Huntsville Division's Private Woodlot Management SCS-RM-00005/COC-00077 SCS Resource Manager Natural 939 ha. Total for Canada 211 013 ha.

Costa Rica

Asosiacion San Miguelena de Conservacion y Desarrollo (ASACODE) SW-FM/COC-056 Rainforest Alliance Non-Industrial Plantation/Semi-natural 81 ha. BALSATICA, S.A SW-FM/COC-060 Rainforest Alliance Private tropical mixed forest 3 500 ha. Corporación Buen Precio, S.A SW-FM/COC-083 Rainforest Alliance Private Plantation 2 662 ha. EcoDirecta, S.A SW-FM/COC-098 Rainforest Alliance Private Plantation 1 121 ha. Flor y Fauna SA SW-FM/COC-06 Rainforest Alliance Industrial Plantation 2 788 ha. Forestales International BV SW-FM/COC-035 Rainforest Alliance Non-Industrial Natural 300 ha. Fundacion para el Desarrollo de la Cordillera Volcanica Central (FUNDECOR) SGS-FM-0056 SGS Forestry Group Plantation/Natural 17 551 ha. Fundacion Tierras Unidas Vecinales por el Ambiente (TUVA) SW-FM/COC-023 Rainforest Alliance Communal Natural 500 ha. Germano-Costarricense, S.A SW-FM/COC-078 Rainforest Alliance Private Plantation 1 200 ha. Portico SA SCS-FM-00003 SCS Industrial Natural 3 946 ha. Reforestation Group International, S.A SW-FM/COC-095 Rainforest Alliance Private Plantation 90 ha. Tropical American Tree Farms (TATF) SW-FM/COC-04 Rainforest Alliance Non-Industrial Plantation 2 629 ha. Total for Costa Rica 36 368 ha.

Czech Republic

Masaryk Forest, Schulforstbetrieb "Masarykuv les" Krtiny SA-FM-1038/COC-1039 Soil Association Government Plantation/Semi-natural 10 441 ha. Total for Czech Republic 10 441 ha.

Denmark

Svejbaekgard I/S SW-FM/COC-094 Rainforest Alliance Private Natural 36 ha. Total for Denmark 36 ha.

Germany

Gemeinde-und Städtebund Rheinland-Pfalz (GStB) FD Koblenz SGS-FM-0224 SGS Forestry Group Semi-Natural 2 933 ha. Gemeinde-und Städtebund Rheinland-Pfalz (GStB) Region rechtsrheinisch IMO-FM/COC-9804 IMO Group Semi-Natural 2 363 ha. Hatzfeldt-Wildenburg'sche Verwaltung SGS-FM-0259 Rainforest Alliance Group Semi-natural 7 320 ha. Landesforstverwaltung SKAL-FM-13479 Skal Government Mixed-natural/plantation 49 236 ha. Naturland Verband e.V. IMO-FM/COC-9887 IMO Group Semi-Natural 13 381 ha. Umweltbehörde Hamburg-Ökologische Forst-und Landwirtschaft SKAL-FM-8521 Skal Government Semi-Natural 4 938 ha. Total for Germany 80 171 ha.

Guatemala

Asociación de Productores de San Miguel (APROSAM) SW-FM/COC-075 Rainforest Alliance Communal Natural 7 039 ha. Comité Pro-Mejoramiento de La Pasadita SW-FM/COC-074 Rainforest Alliance Communal Natural 18 217 ha. Cooperativa Bethel, R.L. SW-FM/COC-076 Rainforest Alliance Communal Natural 4 149 ha. Cooperativa La Técnica Agropecuaria, R.L. SW-FM/COC-073 Rainforest Alliance Communal Natural 4 607 ha. La Sociedad Civil de Impulsores Suchitecos SW-FM/COC-063 Rainforest Alliance Communal Natural 12 217 ha. Total for Guatemala 46 229 ha.

Honduras

La Cooperativa Regional Agroforestal, Colon, Atlántida, Honduras Ltda. SW-FM-024 Rainforest Alliance Resource Manager Natural 7 970 ha. (COATLAHL)Paya y Copén, Colón SW-FM/COC-065 Rainforest Alliance Resource Manager Natural 5 898 ha. Proyecto de Desarrollo del Bosque Latifoliado (PDBL) SW-FM-01 Rainforest Alliance Communal Natural 6 008 ha. Total for Honduras 19 876 ha.

Indonesia

Perum Perhutani: Districts of CEPU, KEBONHARJO AND MANTINGAN SW-FM/COC-053 Rainforest Alliance Government Plantation 62 278 ha. Total for Indonesia 62 278 ha.

Italy

Magnifica Comunita di Fiemme SGS-FM-0071 SGS Forestry Communal Natural 11 000 ha. Total for Italy 11 000 ha.

Malaysia

Deramakot Forest Reserve – Sabah Forestry Department SGS-FM-0065 SGS Forestry Government Natural 55 083 ha. Total for Malaysia 55 083 ha.

Mexico

Ejido Echeverria de la Sierra SW-FM/COC-020 Rainforest Alliance Communal Natural 3 000 ha. El Ejido Colectivo San Juan de Aguinaldos SW-FM-021 Rainforest Alliance Communal Natural 3 000 ha. El Ejido El Centenario SW-FM/COC-052 Rainforest Alliance Communal Natural 2 693 ha. El Ejido Noh Bec SW-FM/COC-066 Rainforest Alliance Communal Natural 23 100 ha. Sociedad Civil de Productores Forestales Ejidales de Quintana Roo (SPFEQR) SW-FM-02 Rainforest Alliance Communal Semi-natural 86 215 ha. Union de Comunidades Forestales Zapotecas-Chinantecas (UZACHI) SW-FM/COC-011 Rainforest Alliance Communal Natural 24 996 ha. Total for Mexico 143 004 ha.

Namibia

Jumbo Charcoal SGS-FM-0219 SGS Forestry Private Natural 49 000 ha. Total for Namibia 49 000 ha.

Netherlands

Dienst Milieu en Openbare Werken Gemeente Arnhem – Sector Stadsbeheer SKAL-FM-8501 Skal Government Semi-natural 1 304 ha. Dienst Openbare Werken Gemeente Ede – Afd. Buurtbeheer SKAL-FM-8503 Skal Government Plantation/Semi-natural 2 044 ha. Gemeente Apeldoorn, Dienst Groen – Natuur en Landschap SKAL-FM-008512 Skal Government Semi-natural 571 ha. Gemeente Lelystad SKAL-FM-8513 Skal Government Plantation/Semi-natural 465 ha. Gemeente Renkum SKAL-FM-8504 Skal Government Plantation/Semi-natural 283 ha. Koninklijke Houtvesterij Het Loo SKAL-FM-8506 Skal Private Plantation/Semi-natural 8 058 ha. Staasbosbeheer Regio Gelderland SGS-FM-0226 SGS Forestry Government Mixed-semi-natural/plantation 16 425 ha. Staatsbosbeheer – Regio Flevoland-Overijssel SKAL-FM-8520 Skal Government Semi-natural 18 200 ha. Staatsbosbeheer – Regio Groningen-Drenthe SKAL-FM/COC-008524 Skal Government Plantation/Semi-natural 21 714 ha. Total for Netherlands 69 064 ha.

New Zealand

Craigpine Timber Ltd. SGS-FM-0096 SGS Forestry Industrial Plantation 2 305 ha. Rayonier New Zealand SGS-FM-0097 SGS Forestry Industrial Plantation 42 720 ha. Total for New Zealand 45 025 ha.

Panama

Futuro Forestal, S.A. SW-FM/COC-037 Rainforest Alliance Non-Industrial Plantation 23 ha. Total for Panama 23 ha.

Papua New Guinea

EU-IRECDP SGS-FM-0169 SGS Forestry Communal Natural 4 310 ha. Total for Papua New Guinea 4 310 ha.

Poland

Regional Directorate of State Forest, Szczecin SGS-FM-0243 SGS Forestry Government Mixed-natural/plantation 612 937 ha. Regional Directorate of State Wroclaw Forests SGS-FM-0177 SGS Forestry Government Natural 511 340 ha. Regional Directorates of State Forests – Gdansk SGS-FM-0007 SGS Forestry Government Natural 298 000 ha. Regional Directorates of State Forests – Krakow SGS-FM-0086 SGS Forestry Government Natural 173 166 ha. Regional Directorates of State Forests – Szczecinek SGS-FM-0008 SGS Forestry Government Natural 622 563 ha. Total for Poland 2 218 006 ha.

Solomon Islands

Kolombangara Forest Products Ltd. SA-FMU-1069/COC-1070 Soil Association Industrial Plantation/Semi-natural 38 000 ha. Soltrust SW-FM/COC-054 Rainforest Alliance Communal Natural 2 450 ha. SWIF with Pari and Assoc. Development Project Head Forestry Silas Teu SGS-FM-0034-0042 SGS Forestry Communal Natural 1 306 ha. SWIFT SGS-FM-0057 SGS Forestry Group Natural 1 106 ha. SWIFT with Paletau and Brothers Eco-Timber Project SGS-FM-0054 SGS Forestry Communal Natural 50 ha. Total for Solomon Islands 42 912 ha.

South Africa

African Charcoal (AFCHAR) Group Certification SGS-FM-0053 SGS Forestry Group Plantation/Natural 1 458 ha. Bracken Timbers SGS-FM-0016 SGS Forestry Industrial Plantation 4 500 ha. Mondi Forests – Northern Region SGS-FM-0084 SGS Forestry Industrial Natural 431 301 ha. South African Forestry Company Ltd. (SAFCOL) – Eastern Cape Region SGS-FM-0123 SGS Forestry Industrial Plantation 42 714 ha. South African Forestry Company Ltd. (SAFCOL) – KwaZulu-Natal Region SGS-FM-0050 SGS Forestry Industrial Plantation 51 922 ha. South African Forestry Company Ltd. (SAFCOL) – Mpumalanga North Region SGS-FM-0112 SGS Forestry Industrial Plantation 64 378 ha. South African Forestry Company Ltd. (SAFCOL) – Mpumalanga South Region SGS-FM-0068 SGS Forestry Industrial Plantation 58 818 ha. South African Forestry Company Ltd. (SAFCOL) – Western Cape Region SGS-FM-0133 SGS Forestry Industrial Plantation 53 530 ha. Total for South Africa 708 621 ha.

Sri Lanka

Parquet (Ceylon) Ltd. – Horana Plantations Ltd. SGS-FM-0045 SGS Forestry Industrial Plantation 2 668 ha. Parquet (Ceylon) Ltd. – RPK Management services (Pvt.) SGS-FM-0046 SGS Forestry Industrial Plantation 5 476 ha. Western CorkLtd: 12 rubberwood plantations SGS-FM-0047 SGS Forestry Industrial Plantation 4 582 ha. Total for Sri Lanka 12 726 ha.

Sweden

AssiDomän Forest and Timber SGS-FM-0269 SGS Forestry Group Mixed-natural/plantation 9 104 ha. AssiDomän Skog & Trä AB – Älvsbyn Region SGS-FM-0082 SGS Forestry Industrial Semi-Natural 676 000 ha. AssiDomän Skog & Trä AB – Hedemora Region SGS-FM-0141 SGS Forestry Industrial Semi-Natural 397 790 ha. AssiDomän Skog & Trä AB – Kalix Region SGS-FM-0083 SGS Forestry Industrial Semi-Natural 778 000 ha. AssiDomän Skog & Trä AB – Lycksele Region SGS-FM-0109 SGS Forestry Industrial Semi-Natural 727 000 ha. AssiDomän Skog & Trä AB – Örebro Region SGS-FM-0073 SGS Forestry Industrial Semi-Natural 256 000 ha. AssiDomän Skog & Trä AB – Östersund Region SGS-FM-0130 SGS Forestry Industrial Semi-Natural 180 000 ha. AssiDomän Skog & Trä AB – Värnamo Region SGS-FM-0110 SGS Forestry Industrial Semi-Natural 141 000 ha. AssiDomän Skog & Trä AB – Växjö Region SGS-FM-0131 SGS Forestry Industrial Semi-Natural 171 000 ha. Graninge Skog Och Tra AB SA-FM-1085 Soil Association 320 000 ha. Körsnas Aktiebolag Skog Gimo, Ljusdal & Dala Reegions SGS-FM-0076 SGS Forestry Industrial Semi-Natural 664 200 ha. MoDo Skog AB SA-FMU-1077 Soil Association Industrial Semi-natural 1 044 000 ha. Saffle Management District of Stora Forest AB SCS-FM-00018 SCS Industrial Semi-Natural 91 000 Sala Kommun SA-FMU-1064 Soil Association Industrial Semi-Natural 5 796 ha. SCA Forest and Timber AB SGS-FM-0213 SGS Forestry Industrial Semi-Natural 1 800 000 ha. Skogssallskapet Förvaltning AB SA-FMU/COC-1057 Soil Association Group Semi-Natural 171 000 ha. Stockholm Vatten SA-FMU-1065 Soil Association Private Semi-Natural 5 543 ha. STORA, Ludvika District SCS-FM-00004 SCS Industrial Semi-Natural 300 000 STORA, Forest AB, Torsby Forest Management District SCS-FM-00020/COC-00104 SCS Industrial Semi-Natural 265 000 ha. STORA, Mora District SCS-FM-00014/COC-00074 SCS Industrial Semi-Natural 300 000 ha. STORA, Söderhamn District SCS-FM-00017 SCS Industrial Semi-Natural 260 000 ha. STORA, Strömsberg District SCS-FM-00015 SCS Industrial Semi-Natural 92 000 ha. STORA, Sveg District SCS-FM-00013/COC-00056 SCS Industrial Semi-Natural 285 000 ha. STORA, Syd District SCS-FM-00019 SCS Forestry Industrial Semi-Natural 12 000 ha. SUSAB SGS-FM-0345 SGS Forestry Group Natural 18 012 ha. Sydved AB SGS-FM-0267 SGS Forestry Group Mixed-natural/plantation 7 000 ha. Västeras Stifts Egendomsförvaltning SA-FMU-1071/COC-1071 Soil Association Non-Industrial Semi-Natural 68 250 ha. Total for Sweden 9 044 695 ha.

Switzerland

Rollirain Foundation IMO-FM/COC-9712 IMO Private Natural 17 ha. Solothurn SGS-FM-0111 SGS Forestry Government Natural 2 095 ha. Waldamt der Stadt Zürich SGS-FM-371 SGS Forestry Government Natural 2 140 ha. Total for Switzerland 4 252 ha.

United Kingdom

Big K Charcoal Merchants Ltd. SA-FM-1014/COC-1015 Soil Association Group Plantation/Semi-natural 739 ha. Clun Valley Alder Charcoal Pilot Project SA-FMU/COC-1107 Soil Association Resource Manager Semi-natural 5 ha. Coed Cymru SGS-FM-0069 SGS Forestry Group Semi-natural 28 600 ha. Dartington Home Woods SA-FM-1002/COC-1013 Soil Association Non-Industrial Plantation/Semi-natural 103 ha. David Goss & Associates SGS-FM-0324 SGS Forestry Resource Manager Natural 9 500 ha. Duchy of Cornwall Woodlands Estate, Phase 1 SA-FM-1018/COC-1019 Soil Association Private Plantation/Semi-natural 254 ha. Duchy of Cornwall Woodlands Estate, Phase 2 SA-FM-1042/COC-1073 Soil Association Private Plantation/Semi-natural 725 ha. Forest Enterprise (England) SGS-FM-0356 SGS Forestry Group Plantation/Semi-natural 218 542 ha. Forest Enterprise (North Scotland) SGS-FM-0354 SGS Forestry Government Plantation/Semi-natural 298 780 ha. Forest Enterprise (S. Scotland) SGS-FM-0355 SGS Forestry Government Plantation/Semi-natural 197 600 ha. Forest Enterprise (Wales) SGS-FM-0357 SGS Forestry Government Plantation/Semi-natural 118 229 ha. Independent Forestry SGS-FM-0238 SGS Forestry Group Plantation/Semi-natural 1 822 ha. Plashett Wood, IV Askew Charitable Trust SA-FM-1024/COC-1025 Soil Association Non-Industrial Semi-natural 150 ha. Scottish Woodlands Ltd. SGS-FM-0260 SGS Forestry Group Natural 2 834 ha. Telford and Wrekin Council SA-FMU-1059/COC-1060 Soil Association Government Plantation/Natural 452 ha. Woodland Trust, The SGS-FM-0150 SGS Forestry Non-Industrial Natural 9 850 ha. Total for United Kingdom 888 185 ha.

United States of America

Applied Forest Management, L.L.C. SCS-RM-00006 SCS Group Natural 8 920 ha. Arcata City Forest SW-FM-040 Rainforest Alliance Government Natural 486 ha. Big Creek Lumber Co. SCS-FM-00009/COC-00002 SCS Industrial Natural 2 720 ha. Blencowe Managed Forest Lands SW-FM/COC-09 Rainforest Alliance Resource Manager Plantation/Natural 4 878 ha. Bohn Family Forest SW-FM/COC-080 Rainforest Alliance Private Natural 65 ha. Brown Tract – managed by Woodland Management Inc. SW-FM/COC-032 Rainforest Alliance Resource Manager Plantation/Natural 120 ha. Chase Mountain Management Corporation SW-FM/COC-071 Rainforest Alliance Private Natural 374 ha. Clarck Forestry, Inc. SW-FM/COC-096 Rainforest Alliance Resource Manager Natural 6 207 ha. Collins Pine – The Collins Almanor Forest SCS-FM-00006/COC-00023 SCS Industrial Natural 37 600 ha. Columbia West Virginia Corporation SW-FM/COC-091 Rainforest Alliance Private Natural 3 985 ha. Darcie Mahoney Forestry SW-FM/COC-034 Rainforest Alliance Resource Manager Natural 353 ha. Ecoforestry Institute: Mountain grove SW-FM/COC-043 Rainforest Alliance Non-Industrial Natural 170 ha. Ecoforestry Management Associates SW-FM/COC-042 Rainforest Alliance Resource Manager Natural 142 ha. Ellis J. Louie & Sons, Butte Ranch Creek SW-FM/COC-055 Rainforest Alliance Non-Industrial Natural 1 416 ha. Forest, Soil, and Water SW-FM/COC-044 Rainforest Alliance Resource Manager Natural 182 ha. Full Cycle Woodworks, Inc. SW-FM/COC-067 Rainforest Alliance Private Natural 1 210 ha. Heartwood Forestland Fund, LP. (Emory River Tract, Morgan County TN The SW-FM/COC-092 Rainforest Alliance Private Natural 12 994 ha. Forestland group, LLC).

Hickman Timber Management SW-FM/COC-064 Rainforest Alliance Private Natural 2 912 ha. Hoopa Valley Tribe SW-FM/COC-068 Rainforest Alliance Communal Natural 34 836 ha. Huff, Eric SCS-RM-00002 SCS Resource Manager Natural 1 497 ha. Individual Tree Selection Management Inc. SW-FM/COC-025 Rainforest Alliance Resource Manager Natural 2 033 ha. J-Spear Ranch Co. SW-FM/COC-069 Rainforest Alliance Private Natural 6 270 ha. Jacobszoon Forestry Consulting SW-FM/COC-026 Rainforest Alliance Resource Manager Natural 1 529 ha. James L. Able Consulting, Inc. SW-FM/COC-059 Rainforest Alliance Private Mixed-natural/plantation 14 165 ha. Jani, Mike SCS-RM-00001 SCS Resource Manager Natural 1 497 ha. Kan Property, The SW-FM/COC-030 Rainforest Alliance Non-Industrial Natural 17 ha. Kane hardwood SCS-FM-00007 SCS Industrial Natural 46 964 ha. Keith Horn, Inc. SW-FM/COC-085 Rainforest Alliance Resource Manager Natural 7 165 ha. Keweenaw Land Association Ltd. SW-FM-05 Rainforest Alliance Industrial Natural 52 845 ha. Krantz-Kahan Property SW-FM/COC-027 Rainforest Alliance Non-Industrial Natural 24 ha. Lakeview Forest – Division of Collins

Products LLC SCS-FM-00012 SCS Industrial Natural 29 150 ha. Lusignan Forestry, Inc. SW-FM/COC-077 Rainforest Alliance Resource Manager Natural 1 309 ha. Marin Municipal Water District (MMWD) SW-FM/COC-084 Rainforest Alliance Communal Natural 81 ha. Mark Andre RPF SW-FM/COC-072 Rainforest Alliance Resource Manager Natural 661 ha. Massachusetts Metropolitan District Commission, Quabbin Reservoir Lands SW-FM/COC-022 Rainforest Alliance Government Natural 21 862 ha. McClellan Mountain Ranch SW-FM/COC-08 Rainforest Alliance Non-Industrial Semi-natural 133 ha. McCloud Tree Farm/Hancock Natural Resource Group, Inc. SW-FM/COC-097 Rainforest Alliance Private Semi-natural 16 181 ha. Menominee Tribal Enterprises Ltd. SW-FM-07/SCS-FM-0002 Rainforest Alliance & Industrial Natural 94 737 ha. Merck Forest and Farmland Center SW-FM/COC-088 Rainforest Alliance Private Natural 1 266 ha. Mid-Maine Forestry SCS-RM-00004/COC-00066 SCS Resource Manager Natural 1 402 ha. Minnesota Aitkin County Land Department SW-FM/COC-028 Rainforest Alliance Government Natural 89 876 ha. Minnesota Department of Natural Resources SW-FM/COC-029 Rainforest Alliance Government Natural 146 719 ha. Nicholas Kent Consulting SW-FM/COC-049 Rainforest Alliance Resource Manager Natural 7 287 ha. Northeast Ecologically Sustainable Timber (NEST) SW-FM/COC-014 Rainforest Alliance Resource Manager Natural 1 360 ha. Our Lady of the Redwoods Inc. SW-FM/COC-017 Rainforest Alliance Non-Industrial Natural 162 ha. Paul Smith's College SW-FM/COC-089 Rainforest Alliance Communal Natural 4 726 ha. Pennsylvania State Forest – Districts 9,10, 12, 13, 15, & 16 SCS-FM-00011 SCS Government Natural 485 633 ha. Red Hills Lumber (formerly Sedgwick Land Company) SW-FM/COC-018 Rainforest Alliance Non-Industrial Natural 2 996 ha. Redtree Properties L.P. SW-FM/COC-057 Rainforest Alliance Non-Industrial Natural 2 865 ha. Restoration Forestry, Inc. SW-FM/COC-082 Rainforest Alliance Resource Manager Natural 682 ha. Robert Whittaker Family Property SW-FM/COC-051 Rainforest Alliance Non-Industrial Natural 1 175 ha. Rocky Creek Ranch/Pondelick Property SW-FM/COC-070 Rainforest Alliance Private Natural 990 ha. Seven Islands Land Management Co – Pingree Family Ownership SCS-FM-00005/COC-00030 SCS Private Natural 394 577 ha. Society for the Protection of New Hampshire Forests SW-FM/COC-062 Rainforest Alliance Private Natural 11 102 ha. Staub, Steve SCS-RM-00003 SCS Resource Manager Natural 91 ha. Still Waters Farm SW-FM/COC-041 Rainforest Alliance Non-Industrial Natural 16 ha. Surface Road Associates SW-FM/COC-016 Rainforest Alliance Non-Industrial Natural 12 ha. Talbert & Nunamaker Forestry Consultants SW-FM/COC-081 Rainforest Alliance Resource Manager Natural 1 120 ha. The Ecosystem Management Company SW-FM/COC-090 Rainforest Alliance Private Natural 1 631 ha. Timbergreen Forestry SW-FM/COC-046 Rainforest Alliance Non-Industrial Natural 405 ha. Tree Shepherd Woods SW-FM/COC-013 Rainforest Alliance Non-Industrial Natural 8 ha. Tunheim, Edward SW-FM/COC-039 Rainforest Alliance Resource Manager Natural 8 094 ha. Two Trees Forestry SW-FM/COC-015 Rainforest Alliance Group Natural 8 096 ha. Vermont Family Forests SW-FM/COC-048 Rainforest Alliance Group Natural 2 666 ha. Whiskey Creek Timber Company SW-FM/COC-079 Rainforest Alliance Private Natural 1 390 ha. Whitney, Bob SCS-FM-00010 SCS Non-Industrial Natural 40 ha. Wylatti Timber Management Company Ltd. SW-FM/COC-012 Rainforest Alliance Non-Industrial Natural 566 ha. Zena Timber SW-FM/COC-061 Rainforest Alliance Private Natural 728 ha. Total for United States of America 1 595 371 ha.

Zambia

NCT Forestry Co-operative Ltd. SGS-FM-0348 SGS Forestry Group Natural 71 000 ha. Total for Zambia 71 000 ha.

Zimbabwe

Border Timbers Ltd. SGS-FM-0293 SGS Forestry Government Plantation 47 654 ha. Durawood Products Ltd – Pumula Forest Area SGS-FM-0001 SGS Forestry Communal Natural 24 850 ha. Total for Zimbabwe 72 504 ha.

Source: FSC Web site: http://www.fscoax.org/principal.htm

FSC-accredited Auditors

THE NETHERLANDS
Skal, Mr.Jan-Willem Heezen, Stationsplein 5, P.O. Box 384, 8000 AJ Zwolle, The Netherlands Tel: +31 38 426 81 81 Fax: +31 38 4213063 E-mail: info@skal.com Website: http://www.Skal.com

SWITZERLAND
Institut für Marktökologie (IMO), Mr. Karl Büchel, Poststrasse 8, CH-8583 Sulgen, Switzerland Tel: +41 71 644 9880 Fax: +41 71 644 9883 E-mail: forest@imo.ch E-mail: office@imo.ch Website: http://www.imo.ch

UNITED KINGDOM
SGS Forestry QUALIFOR Programme, Mrs Ruth Nussbaum, Oxford Centre for Innovation, Mill Street, Oxford OX2 0JX, UK Tel: +44 1865 201 212. Fax: +44 1865 790441 E-mail: forestry@sgsgroup.com Website :http://www.sgs.co.uk/qualifor

Soil Association Woodmark Scheme, Mr. Matthew Wenban Smith, Bristol House, 40-56 Victoria Street, Bristol BS1 6BY, UK Tel: +44 117 914 2435/929 0661 Fax: +44 117 925 2504 E-mail: wm@soilassociation.org Website: http://www.earthfood.co.uk

UNITED STATES
Rainforest Alliance Smart Wood Program, Ms Wendy Hall, #61 Millet Street, Goodwin Baker Building, Richmond, VT 05477, USA Tel: +1 802 434 5491 Fax: +1 802 434 3116 E-mail: smartwood@ra.org E-mail: wjhall@smartwood.org Website:http://www.smartwood.org

Scientific Certification Systems Forest Conservation Program, Ms Debbie Hammel, Park Plaza Building, 1939 Harrison Street, Suite 400, Oakland, CA 94612-3532 USA Tel: +1 510 832 1415 Fax: +1 510 832 0359 E-mail: dhammel@scs1.com Website: http://www.scs1.com